Rev Your
Wife's Engine

Fine Tuning the Mechanics of Wife
Maintenance for a Lifetime of Satisfaction

Cathy Goekler

WESTBOW
PRESS
A DIVISION OF THOMAS NELSON

WestBow Press books may be ordered through booksellers or by contacting:

WestBow Press
A Division of Thomas Nelson
1663 Liberty Drive
Bloomington, IN 47403
www.westbowpress.com
1-(866) 928-1240

Scripture quotations are from The New International Version, The Message, The New Testament in Modern English, and The New Living Translation and are noted in the appendix.

ISBN: 978-1-4908-0415-6 (sc)
ISBN: 978-1-4908-0414-9 (hc)
ISBN: 978-1-4908-0416-3 (e)

Library of Congress Control Number: 2013914206

Printed in the United States of America.

WestBow Press rev. date: 9/16/2013

DEDICATION

To Harold, with love.

To my wonderful children, with love.

To my delightful grandchildren, to my parents,

To my friends and family, with love.

"'The only thing that counts is faith expressing itself through love.'"

To my Father, Brother, and Friend in eternal gratitude.

TABLE OF CONTENTS

LIST OF TABLES

ACKNOWLEDGMENTS

WHERE DO I start? A book on marriage isn't influenced by one person. It's about all the friends in school and their parents, K-12 and beyond. It's about all the young marriages we once were part of. It's about all the faithful friends along the way who have walked with us through our ups and downs. It's about our church families and pastors, our own families, co-workers, and parents. It's about my own marriage. It's about the good examples and the good bad examples. And it's about the faithful writers who have encouraged cajoled, critiqued, and blessed me. It's about publishers who have faith and pursue excellence. It's the material, the process, and the publication.

"Write this down for the next generation so people not yet born will praise God."[1]

It's about my grandchildren, Luke, Vince, Jude, Trace, Jade, Wes, and Drake.

Without my sons, Matt, Travis, and Shandan, this book wouldn't have been inspired.

Without my girls, Joy, Grace, Kara, and Katie, this book wouldn't have made sense.

Without my parents, Gail, Billie, and Joe, this book wouldn't have had heart.

Without all the friends who support me on this journey from Chico to Herlong, Los Gatos, San Luis Obispo, Corvallis, Topeka, Pedee, and Cannon Beach, this book wouldn't have had reality.

Without my family, who have been friends as well, this book wouldn't have roots.

Without my critique group, Ron, Dick, Pamela, Lianne, Carol, Katie, and especially Michael, this wouldn't have been finished.

Without OCW I wouldn't have known what I was doing.

Finally, without my faithful, loyal, loving, kind, by-my-side husband, Harold, this book simply wouldn't be. Thank you, honey.

"Now, to him who by his power within us is able to do far more than we ever dare to ask or imagine - to him be glory in the Church and in Christ Jesus for ever and ever, amen!"[2]

SECTION 1:
INTRODUCTION

CHAPTER 1

Introduction to Your Dodge, Chevy, Ford, Jeep, Mercedes, Or Jaguar Wife

To my sons:

What you are about to read is not politically correct. I'm a mom. I can do this.

After you left home, I realized there were a few holes in your education. One void was understanding women. Do over? I'll try to make this as painless as possible. Let's begin with a story.

Watching Charlton Heston play a schoolmaster in *The Private War of Major Benson* started this project. When one of the boys asks Mr. Heston to explain women, he gives the usual, wrong, and intentionally funny responses. It would be funny if it weren't so true! Then inspiration struck. I realized here was *the* reason men and women don't understand each other! Men ask *men* to explain women! How silly. How can a man explain something he has never been? (Never mind that men sell successful books on pregnancy!) If a guy wants to understand women, he's going to have to go to the source.

The problem is bigger than just telling each other—we already use the same words, but they don't mean the same things. We have to find a common language. Mars and Venus are nice, but none of us has ever been there. You've been into engines since you were little, so could we translate something you don't innately understand (women) into something you do (vehicles)?

Because most guys don't understand women, they tend to toss flowers or candy at them and hope something works. If you have a sputtering engine, buying random new parts, opening the hood, throwing them in, and slamming the hood shut, hoping the problem gets fixed while you wait is pretty silly, huh? Guys react to women that way because they don't have the three benefits they have with cars and trucks. With vehicles, they: receive instruction, invest in tools, and develop skills. Do those three things in marriage and you're on the road to a better relationship.

I hear whining out there. *"Women are too complex."* Guess what? So are vehicles. You don't have to understand physics, engineering, or compression ratios to happily maintain a vehicle, do you? Complexity doesn't stop you from taking care of a vehicle. So the complexity of a woman isn't the real problem. It's a matter of attitude. If you can maintain a vehicle, you can maintain a wife.

You didn't know what you were doing the first time you popped a hood, but you believed you could succeed. That attitude carried you through years of busted knuckles, burns, and frustration. If you choose the same attitude toward understanding your wife, you can have success with her, too.

There's one other problem. One reason guys can be so *without-a-clue* about relationships is the toys we gave you. You had action figures. Girls have Barbie™. Your "guys" come with accessories like trucks and winches. Barbie™ comes with accessories, too. One of them is... *Ken*™. Since childhood, girls have been practicing relationships and guys have been practicing with tools. That's okay—I can't back a trailer worth toast and you and the Fisher-Price™ camper set have been doing it since you were two. Blame being *without-a-clue* on the toys and move on.

Note: This book is only a book, not a magic wand. *You* still have to get the tools, practice the skills, and do the work just as you did with the vehicles.

A few more words about how to use this information: Once upon a time, two guys I know decided to rebuild important parts under the hood of an old green VW bus. They had a few tools, a few instructions, and shiny parts in their boxes. They didn't have a garage, but this was college and neither did anyone else. It was sunny and warm so the street would do. A few hours and a few beers later, *Tadah*! They were satisfyingly dirty and the bus no longer sputtered. The only problem was there were parts left over. Shiny parts. Several, in fact. The guys were certain they belonged *somewhere* under the green hood. They'd followed the directions and hadn't drunk that many beers. Should they take it apart and try again? They shrugged their shoulders and went on with life. If the parts were that important, they'd know about it soon enough. And if the van ran without them, then how important could they really be?

Expect to have parts left over the first time you use these instructions. Give yourself permission to learn, to do-over when necessary. When you buy a vehicle manual, you don't read it cover to cover and do everything listed. You use it as you need it. Use this handbook the same way.

Plan to record information in each chapter so it becomes a customized reference book that's specific to your wife. You're meant to refer to it over and over again. You're meant to use it with your bride, but I'm writing it for *you*. Whether or not to read this book is <u>not</u> an option. <u>Do not</u> have her read it and tell you what it's about.

Why is all this necessary? When you purchase a vehicle, you know what you're getting—make, model, engine size, and cargo space. When you marry a woman, her details are unknown. People don't come with manuals. People change. You have to work with that fact and not reduce relationship to a set of rules that never changes in fifty years.

One more thing—here's a pop quiz. What's your VIN? Driver's license number? Oil type? Mileage of the last oil change? Time. Put down your pencils.

Although you likely didn't get one hundred-percent, I bet you know where to find the information. You're not a bad car owner because you don't remember all this stuff. You don't use it every day, so you tend to forget. The point is that you keep a record of it so when it's needed, you've got it. In the same way, you're not a bad husband because you don't remember every detail about your wife. Use this book to store the information you don't use every day. Don't guess. Ask. *Her input is crucial to get accurate information.* Once you have the information, use it.

One final note: vehicle manuals come with notes, cautions, and warnings. The same format is used here for the same reason: failure to heed them means potential pain and suffering.

Okay, let's get started.

CHAPTER 2

Looking Under the Hood Or, What Makes Her Run?

REMEMBER THE FIRST time you popped the hood of your truck? You know there's stuff that could really hurt you, but the risk was worth it. The things lurking under the hood could kill you, but they don't because you learned to respect them. The same is true with your wife. Learn to respect her systems and the two of you will get along just fine. Let's take a quick peek at what's under her hood.

Like your vehicle, women have two sources of energy: stored (batteries) and combustible (fuel). A guy has to pay attention to both systems and know when to add fuel and when to add water. If she can't turn over in the morning, her reserves are likely shot. Adding fuel won't help. Reserves are individual. Some are deep cycle, some are marine, some are twelve months, and some are sixty months. Her level of reserves can change over the years. Reservoirs need to be recharged every time they're used. When the system is working correctly, you don't have to do anything. You just have to notice.

Even though women store energy, they still need fuel and need it often. Fuel capacity is set. You can't get mad at a twelve gallon tank for not holding sixteen gallons. But you can get more efficient at using the fuel available. For now, just know that you have to check two systems and they require different solutions.

You're responsible for the refueling. You don't have to make the fuel, but you have to make sure she gets filled up again. Learn her capacity and her fuel grade. Is she a diesel? Does she need high-grade fuel or regular? Trying to substitute one type for the other doesn't work. You have to know these things. How? We'll cover that in Chapter 12.

Fuel needs to be filtered or it tends to choke off power. And a charged battery can't substitute for an empty fuel tank. All the spark in the world doesn't matter if there's no fuel to ignite.

Then there are electronics—wiring, fuses, and relays. All the connected systems you see under the hood have parallels in your relationship with the woman you love. Electronics communicate information to the driver, to other drivers, and to the engine. Your wife has a complex system of communication as well. It's both internal and external. It depends on more than one system of energy. Battery, fuses, and generator; they're all interdependent. The battery's useless without the generator and vise versa.

Communication helps her see when the going gets dark. Communication helps her back up safely and signal changes in direction. It keeps her warm and fills the air with music. There's a lot riding on electronics! There's a lot riding on communication. It pays to get to know how to keep it in good working order. Good communication is both something you maintain and something you need to tune up regularly.

When you got married, you had certain expectations about the marriage. You wanted it to last, to be happy. One reason so many marriages fail is because individuals don't know what steps to take to achieve their goal. In order to have a good marriage you have to define what you mean by "good" and "marriage." The definition of a good marriage is not the same for everyone. Once it's defined, then the steps become more obvious. You are free to work out your own definition, but you have to actually *do* it. We'll cover the details in Maintenance and Tune-ups.

Remember the story of working on the VW van in the street? You're older than that now. You have a garage. But the garage gets cluttered. In order to have successful maintenance and tune-ups, you have to spend time clearing the clutter. Remember the old computer maxim—GIGO (garbage in, garbage out)? You have to deal with the old stuff that came across the threshold with you. Refusing to de-clutter makes the work you have to do more difficult. Typically, we blame the work for being difficult instead of admitting that we failed to prepare to work.

Garage clutter typically fits into seven major categories.

Clutter #1: Love.

Everyone's definition of love is different. Individual definitions are formed based on personal experience, personality, values, and goals. Everyone wants to do their best in marriage. However, you can be sincere and still be wrong. Unfortunately, your best includes baggage. That leaves us with choices about our baggage: rebel, acknowledge, or deny. We usually do a bit of all three.

Start your engines with a common definition of love:

Love is patient, and kind.
> *Love is not envious, boastful, proud or self-seeking.*
> *Love is not easily angered, and keeps no record of wrongs.*
> *Love does not delight in evil.*
Love celebrates truth, always protects, trusts, hopes, perseveres.
Love never fails.[1]

We all fail at this kind of love. We all inherited weaknesses from our parents, but either we use our inheritance as an excuse or as an opportunity. You can change an inheritance into a legacy. You're both going to have to work at changing the way you love to fit this definition. We all suffer from the *"If you really loved me, you would…"* mentality. Be kind and gentle with each other. Love is very tough, but hearts can be broken.

How we handle failure to love brings us to **Clutter # 2: Baggage.**

Most of the baggage we bring with us has its root in a failure to love. Judging and condemning come more naturally than loving does, especially when we've been hurt. Rebellion and denial cost both of you. This isn't a running-out-of-fuel problem. This is cracking-the-block stuff. Choose to have an attitude of solving and re-solving issues instead of ignoring them or demanding to be right. Know that you may find consensus, only to have the problem arise again under different circumstances. If the problem comes back again, you're going to have to solve it again, as many times as it takes. The challenge is to do so in love.

Think of this as a problem that blows a fuse—you can replace the fuse over and over or you can find the short and solve the problem so you don't blow a fuse. Your choice.

Note: If you choose to do nothing, you're still choosing. If you choose not to change the oil, the problem doesn't magically go away. It won't go away in your life either. We're a family of over-comers. Your heritage is strong. Hand life off to the next generation in good shape so they can run with it. Strength doesn't come easy. The ones before you sacrificed to pass on what strengths they had. You do the same.

Note: In all this call to excellence, please also accept Grace. If any generation could attain perfection and pass it on, we'd have world peace by now. In the real world, we simply need to do the best we can with what we have when the opportunity comes and still love each other. Remember, "*The only thing that counts is faith expressing itself in love.*"[2] (emphasis mine)

CAUTION: Saying, "*I don't ever want to do that again.*" doesn't mean I won't ever do that again. It may only mean I don't want to get caught or pay the consequences, not necessarily that I've decided to change my behavior. Your communication with each other needs to address the blindness we have toward ourselves. Develop the skill and discipline to lovingly call each other on inherent dishonesty and rebellion. Why?

Clutter #3: Honesty.

Because we don't really repent of some of our sins. We stop having sex outside marriage because we get married, not because we confronted the attitudes and small daily choices that inevitably led us to such a choice. We want something better for our children, but they observe those small choices we model and come to the same conclusion we did at their age.

We wonder why they act that way when we "taught" them that sex outside marriage is wrong.

We taught the rule apart from the discipline necessary to achieve it. We modeled small daily choices of rebellion and disobedience while expecting obedience. *"Do what I say, not what I do"*, simply doesn't work. The seed we sow yields true fruit. We need honesty with each other in order to have any hope of knowing why we end up where we do. True love means lovingly telling the truth and then walking the consequences together.

NOTE: CAUTION: WARNING: I said *lovingly*. We'll disappoint, anger, betray, and deny the very ones we love. If venting anger were healthy, every wife beater would be a portrait of serenity. Stuffing anger isn't the solution either. *"Go ahead and be angry. You do well to be angry—but don't use your anger as fuel for revenge. And don't stay angry. Don't go to bed angry. "*[3] I didn't say it was easy. Revenge is easy but it's also sin. Rudeness is sin. Chilling silence is sin. The problem with being angry is that we often do to the other person exactly what they did to us! If it's so wrong, then why did we just do it?

Honesty is healthy. *"I'm so hurt by what you did/said"* is a true, honest statement. *"You're a jerk and I never want to see you again. Don't touch me or talk to me ever again."* may also be true and still not be honest.

There are times we all need help being honest. Some mistakes are like passing gas. Everyone knows something happened. It's embarrassing. Sometimes we need help to fess up. Sure it's best to fess up on your own. King David didn't fess up about Bathsheba for a year and then only after being confronted with his deeds.[4] The goal is to make everyone as comfortable as possible. Freshen the air with your apology and move on. Choose a signal for the two of you—candle, magnet, note, or whatever. The candle, or whatever you choose, means, *"I did something that stinks today and need help talking about it."*

I know this sounds silly. Everyone guards against the obvious big things that hurt a marriage. It's the little things that quietly erode the relationship and eventually kill it. You have a relationship worth fighting for. Just remember, most often the opposition to your marriage comes from within, not without. You have to overcome your own temptations and weaknesses.

And that brings us to **Clutter #4: Anger.**

You have to avoid anger and revenge to restore the relationship to a healthy balance. When you're angry, you have to choose to want the relationship more than you want to retaliate, be right, or vent. Anger usually leads to blame and blame leads to avoiding responsibility. *"For we are each responsible for our own conduct."*[5] Help each other choose wisely. Because you are male and female, you will approach anger differently.

That brings us to **Clutter #5: Gender.**

The most important piece of clutter is the gender stuff. You can't have a healthy relationship if you harbor grime in your attitudes toward women. Underlying all the agendas and heated talk about any bias is an incident. The incident involved people with names. Hold those people accountable for injustice, not the entire gender. Trafficking in stereotypes only avoids communication. In marriage, communication is essential. Stereotypes aren't truth.

Gender bias means we think we're better than another person. When you're married to a woman and think women are inferior to men, you're going to have trouble. Marriage unites two people as one. If you're unequal, you walk with a limp, and you're the one limping. What's worse, the limp is self-induced. Marriage is hard enough without crippling yourself with a bad attitude toward women. You have to give up the jokes about how dumb women are. You have to quit sitting in on or adding to gripe sessions with the guys. See jokes and griping as grinders with a steel carbide blade, capable of grinding away your relationship with your wife. A few laughs with the guys aren't worth it.

Clutter #6: Expectations.

One more bit of clutter. This book is not about getting what you want. If you go into a relationship to get what you want, your relationship is in trouble from the start. I'm explaining how to take care of what you have, how to do your best. That means you have to have an attitude of giving, not getting.

"Husbands, go all out in your love for your wives, exactly as Christ did for the church—a love marked by giving, not getting. Christ's love makes the church whole. His words evoke her beauty. Everything he does and says is designed to bring the best out of her, dressing her in dazzling white silk, radiant with holiness. And that is how husbands ought to love their wives. They're really doing themselves a favor—since they're already "one" in marriage."[6]

Clutter #7: Attitude.

Most guys think their wives are high maintenance. They view relationship work as over the top. Random flowers and candy ought to do it and if they actually *do* some relationship work, they want a great deal of affirmation. That's like wanting high fives all around because you filled the gas tank.

Don't get me wrong. There are high maintenance women out there and their men do deserve praise for doing the work. High maintenance or not, once the girl comes home with you, maintenance is your responsibility. There are more men avoiding their responsibility than there are high maintenance women.

It's a no-brainer that the more regular the maintenance, the more time you get to spend enjoying the vehicle. The same is true with your wife. Making time to maintain your marriage directly benefits you, just as taking care of your vehicle does. Trips, time, and money spent on counselors equate to down time in the shop. There are a lot more fun ways to spend life together. You need to accept that maintenance is not an unreasonable expectation *and* that you can learn how to do it well.

Conclusion

Vehicles come in many styles. So do women. The questions asked about what women want and don't want are silly. You aren't married to "women" or even "woman." You're married to one woman. You need to know what *she* wants and what *she* means. You're not married to the Average Woman any more than she is married to the Average Man. How silly for everyone to be unhappy because the average guy spends four hours a day watching the TV and you prefer to spend your time in the shop. Be yourselves. When you look under the hood, you're getting to know your very own particular engine. Stay there. Listen to her.

Note: Remember this is a manual. Vehicle manuals repeat the same things many times over. All the above will be covered again in more depth in later maintenance checks and tune-ups. For now, keep it simple.

Note: Just because you've cleaned the garage once doesn't mean it's going to stay that way. When the relationship has problems, do a quick scan of these seven areas and see if clutter has accumulated again. We all have different clutter levels. There's isn't a right or wrong here. You need consensus with your bride about what constitutes clutter. Discuss and choose how much clutter is okay for the both of you, then realize you have to hold that agreement lightly. People change and so may clutter tolerance. Be willing to renegotiate your levels.

Steps

1. Go for a ride together (or a walk). Discuss times you've rebelled in the past. Share your baggage. Discuss areas you think you might have trouble giving up your independence. Listen to how your mate feels about being left out of those choices.

2. Make a promise to each other about how you want to handle issues so they don't pile up and crack the block of your marriage. Write it down in this book. Date it.

3. Discuss how you have handled conflict in the past. Share the times you felt were successful and why. Share the times you blew it and why.

Discuss how your honesty is challenged by conflict. Discuss how you want to handle conflict in your marriage. Write it down in this book. Date it.

4. Make a gauge for yourselves for when you need to talk. It isn't complicated—just something you both recognize as a signal for the need to talk. It may be a candle you light, a magnet you stick on the fridge, or a clothespin on a towel in the bathroom. I don't care what you do—just make it work for you. It's better to have some silly gimmick that helps you discuss difficult things than to blow your marriage. Write it down.

5. Discuss how you'll help each other choose the relationship over the urge to anger or revenge. Write it down in this book. Date it.

6. Each of you, on separate pieces of paper, write down the definition of love from Clutter #1. Carry it with you in your wallet/purse in the money section. Review it often enough so every time you reach into your wallet you're reminded of what your love for her is supposed to look like. Don't beat yourself up when you fail.

Tool

1. *"For we are each responsible for our own conduct."*[5] Practice taking responsibility instead of using excuses. It's your multi-purpose tool.

CHAPTER 3

Vehicle Identification Numbers
Or, How Do I Tell What I Have?

THERE ARE ALL sorts of makes and models out there. We tend to choose the one that fits our lifestyle. No matter how attractive that Ferrari is, if you live in the woods at the end of a gravel road, forget it. It's possible to bring the flashy model home and discover, too late, that it can't make it down the driveway. It isn't a matter of *won't*, it's a matter of *can't*. These kinds of relationships are often forged on gambling junkets to Las Vegas and, of course, don't apply to you. But you may have a friend who…

Then there's the matter of maintenance. When Grandma was looking at buying a restored Jag, she was told that when the manual says maintenance is to be performed at 3,000 miles, it meant 3,000 miles. Go one more mile and you'll pay for it. Similarly, some wife models require exacting levels of maintenance, some don't. The Jag isn't being difficult, it's just being a Jag. If you bought a Jag, you bought the maintenance. Don't whine.

Note: Regular maintenance is *not* the same as high maintenance. The Haynes manual on my old van is 408 pages long. The routine maintenance section is *44 pages* long! Just because you don't like to change the oil doesn't make it an unreasonable expectation.

WARNING: Crisis drives change, but it isn't a healthy way to do business with cars or marriages. It means running out of gas at inconvenient times and places, overheating the engine, or failing brakes. It isn't called deferred maintenance. It's called neglect. People and cars don't always recover.

CAUTION: It's *not* advisable to commit to your bride and then bring her home intending to modify her. Chevy parts aren't interchangeable with Jag parts. You shopped all available models before the purchase and found the best out there. Work with the one you got. Putting Ford floor mats in a Ferrari won't make her able to go 4 x-ing.

WARNING: You can get in real trouble taking this simile too far. Women often don't look at vehicles the same way you do. Telling her she reminds you of a Cummins Diesel won't get you the come-hither look. Even though to you it means she can go anywhere, count on her to be by your side, not to break down when the going gets tough and that you love that about her, to her it means she's boxy. Even your explanation won't matter. Trust me.

WARNING: Don't marry project cars. See Dr. Laura's book, *10 Stupid Things Men Do To Mess Up Their Lives*. When you marry a project, your goal is to fix or help. Once they're fixed, you lose interest. If they never get fixed, you get frustrated. Either way, they no longer interest you and you want to get a new project. Solve problems, not people.

See also *10 Stupid Things Women Do To Mess Up Their Lives*. Why? Because you need to know the patterns of the women who mess you up! When hubby and I were dating we went through both of these books and discussed where we saw ourselves. It's a great exercise for marriage because you see just how bad it can get unless you take care of issues while they're small.

I mentioned in the last chapter setting goals. Too many guys think getting married is what marriage is all about. Once "*I do*" is spoken, marriage gets submerged and the job becomes the focus. Too many of you put lots of effort into winning the maiden's hand and then quit the field. The goal was to get married. If you don't change the goal to *staying* married, you won't.

So what should the goal be? That's up to the two of you. You'll work on it lots in this manual. Why? You'll find some goals aren't realistic. You change over the years. Your circumstances change. You may start out wanting a good marriage. You're going to have to define what "good" means to the two of you. You may want a strong marriage or a healthy one. They all mean different things and the two of you need to agree on what you want.

Goals aren't wishes or dreams. Goals are defined by concrete steps and a time frame. If you can't figure out the steps to achieve your goal, then you may have written down a wish instead. Go back and figure out what the real goal is. The reason so few people have enduring marriages is because few people make marriage a priority.

Remember how clumsy you felt the first time you used a tool? You kept using it until you felt confident. The same principle applies here. The first few times you use the tools in this manual won't be as productive as they will be after some practice. If you're dedicated to being the best husband you can be (there's a goal), then you'll keep at this until you're proficient. Don't whine. You can do this.

So—you have to dedicate yourself to taking care of what you have, and decide the route you're going to take (goals). But you can't take care of her if you don't know what model she is. Unlike vehicles, women don't have identification labels tattooed front, back, and side. You have to figure it out. What tools do you use? Personality type, values, and goals. These letters and words are her VIN. Know them.

Most conflict comes from ignorance or improper use of one of these tools. We'll refer to this information in almost every chapter because it's that important. Figure out a way to make this information a part of your daily life. Make it a password, a code, a username. Put it in your wallet in the money section. Get creative.

Tool #1: Personality Type.

There are several tools out there to help you understand personality, just as Craftsman, Bosch, and Milwaukie vie to help you out in the shop. I enjoy using the DISC® personality method[1] on a daily basis because it's quick and easy. When hubby and I do a tune-up, we tend to use Keirsy[2] because it gives us more information. It's the difference between an adjustable wrench and a socket set. If you don't like to do a job, you usually invest in the cheapest tool. Unfortunately, cheap tools usually make the job more difficult. If you don't like a job, then invest in the best tools because they get you back on the road more quickly.

Whatever tool you use, know there are four basic personality types. DISC® and Keirsy[3] use letters to describe them. Other systems use names like sanguine, melancholy, choleric or phlegmatic. Gary Smalley[4] uses word pictures like otter, beaver, lion, and golden retriever. Use whatever works. Feel free to try different tools until you find the one that works for you. Use the charts in Appendix III.

Specific use of these tools is covered in later chapters. For now, just know that personality has four parts: introvert/extrovert, and task/people focus. Two parts are fairly consistent at birth. Two parts flex as you mature. All four parts begin to gel into distinct personality somewhere in your twenties. At your age, you aren't dealing with set-in-stone traits. You're molding them in each other and in yourselves. You will mold each other more than your parents did. Be wise and be gentle.

Take the personality test that appeals the most to you. Do it on your own online. Do it with your wife as a date. Buy one of the books in Appendix II. Consider the book a tool. Take the test however it works for you—just be sure to actually *do* it. It isn't pass-fail; there's no grade. You win just by taking the test.

Tool #2: Values.

Values are another part of her VIN. Know what they are for both of you and you're miles down the road to understanding what makes her tick and how to get her back on track when she needs your help.

Values aren't like personality. They change as we go through life. Values are reflective of personality. That's why you need to know both of them and why they're both part of her VIN. Values change because they help us adjust to changes in life. Since they change, they must be checked, like engine coolant or battery fluid. Go for a truck ride. Take the values test along and do it together. Then discuss which values you chose and what they mean to you. Personality and values drive the third part of her VIN: goals.

Tool #3: Goals.

A goal defines where you want to go. You both need individual goals and goals for your marriage. Not having a goal for your marriage means it has no driver and will roll to the lowest available point. Remember what I said earlier? The goal wasn't to get married. Two people can co-exist for a long time without goals, but the relationship will not be mutually satisfying. The reality is, if you don't have your own goals, you're fulfilling someone else's. Choose wisely.

Goals, like values, change. Goals are difficult to define correctly. The presence of conflict can be the dashboard dummy light for a poorly defined goal. We'll keep coming back to goals throughout the manual, so don't worry about making a list right now. Knowing personality type and values helps set realistic and achievable goals.

WARNING: Do *not* put her on a to-do list. She doesn't want to be something crossed off as being "done."

It's okay to have a five, ten, and fifty-year plan, just as your car does when it goes from break-in to 100,000 miles. Think about it, but don't obsess over it. Remember, this is a new tool and it'll take practice to get the most out of it. For now, start with a plan for this year.

Her VIN is something to keep written down and refer to regularly. I don't expect you to remember it. I do expect you to use it.

You're doing great. Keep going. It gets easier from here.

Steps

1. Take the DISC® personality test (See Appendix III). Write down your types on the form at the end of this chapter in the space provided. Date

it. Share with each other what it means to be that type. Remember, this is a tool for you to use, not a label to bind you.

2. Take the Values test in Appendix III. Date it. Write down the results on the forms at the end of this chapter. Share with each other what it means to have those values. Remember that nobody's right and nobody's wrong.

3. Fill out the Goal sheet in Appendix III for yourself and your marriage. Date it. Write the goals down on the forms at the end of this chapter. Share with each other why you chose them. Relate them to personality and values. Discuss ways you can help each other achieve those goals. Discuss how your goals might cause conflict.

Tools

"Everything you are and think and do is permeated with Oneness. But that doesn't mean you should all look and speak and act the same."[5]

Keep perspective

It's an old joke…the reason men like women to wear leather is that it makes them smell like a new truck…

MY WIFE'S VIN:

Personality Type: _____

Values

1.

2.

3.

4.

5.

Goals

1.

2.

MY VIN:

Personality Type: _____

Values

1.

2.

3.

4.

5.

Goals

1.

2.

CHAPTER 4

Buying Parts Genuine, Factory Authorized, and After- Market Or, Why She Didn't Want Flowers

Now THAT YOU know what you have, you begin to understand what parts are specific to your wife. All parts are obviously not the same. You don't get mad at the Chevy™ because the Mercedes™ part doesn't fit. Your wife's make, model and VIN are just as specific as your vehicle's.

Parts for your wife come in two categories: replacement for what wears out and upgrades. Upgrades can be anything from jewelry to nails, clothing, spas, schools, or vacations, or none of the above. Not all upgrades suit all model wives. Think about it—wheels on a Mini Cooper look silly on a truck. You have a specific model. Begin to look at upgrades with the same discernment you use in looking at wheels.

The great news about upgrades is that you can have them done at Factory Authorized Dealers instead of having to do the work yourself. Where do you find Factory Authorized Dealers? Ask your wife. She has favorite stores. She has favorite catalogues. Ask her to mark the things she drools over in a catalogue. Be sure to also ask her to tell you *why* she chose each item.

Case in point: I have a small stuffed Eeyore® above my computer. If my husband didn't know why I kept that donkey there, he could wrongly assume that I wanted to collect small stuffed animals or that I really like Winnie the Pooh® characters. Both assumptions are wrong. Eeyore® is there because he doesn't take up much space and because he reminds me as I write that God can speak through any old donkey.[1]

Factory Authorized Parts and Dealers: (have her fill in)

Favorite Catalogues:

Favorite Stores:

Favorite Clothes:

Favorite Accessories:

Favorite Flowers:

Favorite Candy:

Favorite Jewelry:

Favorite Books:

Favorite Restaurants:

Favorite Spas:

Favorite Hair/Nail Salon:

Favorite Latte Hangout:

Favorite Sport:

Other Favorites:

If she has lots of ideas under some category, don't get depressed thinking you have to do every one. Think of all those options as one large bull's-eye. The more ideas she gives you, the bigger the bulls-eye. You're building a manual specific to your wife. There are thousands of parts on any vehicle. Let your wife give you many choices so neither of you gets bored.

Upgrades are parts not absolutely essential to the vehicle. Replacement parts are *essential*. Parts of your wife's life will get worn out and need replacement. This is a need, not an option. When signs of wear appear, it's time to replace. Don't wait for the breakdown. When one part breaks, it often breaks other parts. Replacement costs are much higher.

Replacement parts come in two types: Factory Authorized, and Genuine. The same guideline applies here: make sure the part suits your particular model and have her tell you where the part has to come from. Her input on parts is the same as your vehicle's. You pop the hood or check the manual, look up what part number is already there, and then get a replacement to match. Once you know what you're looking for, you know whether you go to Napa or the Ford dealer. Looking up the part number is the same as asking your wife. Once you have *her* part number, then you know where you have to go to get the part.

What kind of parts wear out relatively fast? On a vehicle they're things like clutch components, exhaust systems, or parts for the brakes. The systems that help your wife switch gears, filter out the bad stuff, or stop and go also wear out. You'll learn more about replacement parts in Tune-ups. For now, just realize and accept that some parts wear out fast and need to be replaced often. *Need. Often.* If you accept this trait in your vehicle, please accept it in your wife. Remember, we're talking brakes and clutches here, not the LED in the glove box.

Any discussion of parts brings us to warranties. Don't we wish we all had them? Sending your model back to the manufacturer isn't an option. Factory recalls don't work either. If you're frustrated, then read one of the tune-up chapters that fit your situation.

A final word: have fun building the parts list with your wife. Remember to update it often. The twenty-year old model you began with is not going to have the same tastes when she's forty. She's going to grow up. So are you. Don't keep her in a box because you don't want to make changes. If you don't deal with the changes, wear accelerates and break-downs come more often. You can do this.

CHAPTER 5

Techniques, Tools, and Working Facilities
Or, Don't Do It in the Parking Lot

WHAT GIVES YOU such confidence under the hood? TOOLS! Yessir—armed with little more than a gear-puller, a manual, and absolutely *no* experience, you feel confident you can have this baby back up and running in no time. Guess what—it's the same with relationships. All you need is a manual and some tools and you, too, can successfully rebuild relationships.

Like a car, relationships break down and parts wear out. It's inevitable, not a negative reflection on either one of you. Even with a perfect maintenance schedule, things wear out. People change. After 40,000 miles you *need* to pop the hood and look a little deeper than gas, tires, and oil. You have to invest time, money, and resources. Check the belts, grease the bearings, and rotate the tires. Plan for marriage maintenance the way you plan for your 40,000 mile check-up and it won't be so painful.

Relationships come with a guarantee. Skip the routine maintenance, either the weekly stuff or the scheduled big stuff, and your marriage engine will start missing. Unmaintained belts develop squeals and whines. So does your wife. The engine, like the marriage, doesn't "suddenly" go snap. The problems were there all along. You just didn't listen to them. Ignoring small signals leads to louder and louder protesting sounds until the brakes fail or the engine blows.

All the tools in the world are useless if you never learn how to use them. The more you use them, the more efficient and capable you become. It's just as true under the hood as it is with your wife. Knowing which tool to use, and when, is the key. Let's look at a few common tools.

Tool #1: Ears.

Technique #1: Listening.

Goal: To gather information.

The language of men and cars is filled with noises—ping, knock, squeal, squeak, grind, rattle, tick. You listen all the time. You diagnose an engine based on what you hear. You know what it's supposed to sound like so it only takes a moment to know if something's wrong.

Note: Listening alone doesn't give you all the answers, either with the engine or with a wife. What you hear determines what action you take. A click means "check the electrical," a squeal, "check the belts." Learn to hear and interpret the sounds of your wife.

Women speak volumes, just like the engine does. The entire time you're behind the wheel, your little darling is humming along under the hood. She's speaking to you. You don't drive while listening constantly. You start the engine, proceed to fire up the tunes or roll down the window. The same principle applies here—if you regularly listen, she feels heard and you both get on your way.

Listening techniques don't require long hours sitting on the couch each day doing nothing but listening with your eyes rolling to the back of your head. You listen while the engine is doing things. Listen to her while she's doing things. Listen for the sigh, the slam, the bang, the stomp. Do it as often with your wife as you do each time you're in the vehicle.

When you were little, you were taught three words to recite before crossing the street—stop, look, and listen. The same sequence holds true here. The most important maintenance technique you'll need to master is the ability to listen. You have to *stop* doing whatever, *look* at her (not through her or around her to the TV screen), and *listen*. The listening skill you have with your vehicle is transferable to listening to your wife. You can do this.

Note: Girls—don't overwhelm him with words—this isn't permission for you to babble on forever. Remember that wonderful proverb? *When words are many, sin is not absent, but he who holds his tongue is wise.*[1] Guys—you have to teach her your word level. This is where authorized parts are necessary for both genders. To tell your wife she can't talk is to bind her up in knots. It's cruel. She has to talk. You're free to tell her when the best times are for you to listen. Then do it.

Technique #2: Places to listen.

When you were dating, you did a lot of talking and listening. You usually did it while on a date, in the car, over dinner, or on a hike. If it worked for you while dating, then it makes sense to keep it up. I love truck talks because when one part of your brain is occupied, the creative side opens up. Ideas, dreams, solutions to problems start flowing. Truck rides aren't for everyone. It puts some people to sleep. Do whatever worked for you while dating.

Note: Truck talks are used for routine maintenance, *not* conflict resolution. If the conversation gets bumpy, apply one of two techniques. Either stop the vehicle and talk, or agree to table the topic until you reach an appropriate facility (probably home).

The point is you have to schedule maintenance just like you do with Goodyear. You work it into your schedule. You arrange transportation while they work on your vehicle, or, you sit there and eat stale popcorn. You get the job done.

Technique #3: Reading.

Read a marriage book together on a regular basis. Remember the goal is to listen. A marriage book is like putting the engine on the computer and getting a read-out. You don't have to act on or agree with everything the computer says. The reason you have that power is because you listened and evaluated. Reading a marriage book together does the same thing for you.

You choose your own definition of "a regular basis," maybe once a year, plus or minus 20,000 miles, depending on how hard the engine is used. Hubby and I tend to take a book on a weekend getaway. I read while he drives. I read until either of us has something to say, then we discuss. We stop when we're tired. The goal is *not* "finish the book." If that were the case it wouldn't matter what we learned. The goal is to get something out of the book that helps us have a better marriage. We don't make an issue out of who chooses the book. Either of us can, but we both look it over and agree to which one we actually read.

Appendix II has a list of recommended books and resources, by no means complete or exhaustive. If you don't like what you see, you're free to find something that works for both of you.

Technique #4: Conferences.

One of the blessings of getting older is that you see more clearly what you could have done differently. Attending marriage conferences is one of those belated wisdoms. Going away for a weekend gets you away from distractions and lets you focus on working on what needs to be done. You don't try to replace head gaskets on the same weekend as Super Bowl Sunday, the Ferrari rally, and the Foster Mud Flats Races. You can't listen if you're distracted. Focus on each other and learn from the pros.

Technique #5: Regular Dating.

When I know I'm going to have a chance to talk every week, then I don't get anxious about how or when to bring up a topic. Because I'm not anxious about timing, I more easily share what needs to be aired. Regular dates are as important as the brakes or oil in your relationship. Properly maintained they keep things running smoothly. Not checking them means squeals, failure, and explosions. Checking is the key. You don't change the oil and filter every time you check it. You don't bleed the brakes every time you check the brakes. Regular dates are simply keeping an eye on what matters.

You and your bride need to define what you mean by "regular" and "dating." Dating is expensive. So is changing the oil. Failure to do either means greater cost down the road. Dating is supposed to be fun for both of you. Your definition depends on your wife-model. It'll change as you age. The places you went for entertainment when you were sixteen aren't as thrilling when you're forty. Learn to adjust.

Dates don't have to cost. I consider a truck ride or an evening walk a date. Why? Because it gives us quality time together. Talking happens. I look forward to it every day. The truck ride might be a trip to get the mail. Dinners and movies are nice, but they get old much more quickly than an evening walk. Remember, dates are a listening technique. Make your routine dates inexpensive. You don't want to give up dating because you can't afford it.

WARNING: Avoid the term "cheap date."

Also plan for special dates. You don't want to get in a rut. Take turns planning them. Be a good date when it's her turn to plan. Special dates don't have the same function as regular dates. Special dates are celebrations. Regular dates are for listening. You wouldn't have won her hand if you didn't make and keep regular dates. You would have drifted apart. You _will_ drift apart in marriage if you don't continue dating.

Tool #2 Fasteners: Commitment.

Technique #1: Commit to marriage.

Goal: Keep the marriage together during rough roads.

Almost all fasteners use a locking device of some kind to hold two or more parts together. I know you already said, "I do." Sometimes we need to review what that means as the years go by. We need something outside ourselves to keep a marriage together; otherwise, marriages are based on feelings and feelings change. Sometimes it's easy to respect a person. Other times it isn't. When you can't, you have to honor the institution the person represents, otherwise you quit waaaay too soon.

A trucker was going down I-84 during one of the famous Columbia Gorge storms. The road was icy, driving was hazardous. The trucker got scared and opened his door, ready to jump if he lost control. A fellow trucker CB-ed, "Either jump or drive."

By the same token, as long as you think there's a way out, you won't be looking for ways to make marriage work. Marriage can be very hazardous. You can't drive safely if you're only part way in the driver's seat.

Technique #2: Commit to Conflict Resolution.

The process of conflict resolution is covered during Tune-up #4. The technique to practice and use is *being committed to resolution*. Commitment means the small irritant and the big disagreement are both worth your time and effort. The thing about fasteners is that they rust, they wear out. You don't replace a worn fastener with another worn fastener. When you don't replace worn or rusted fasteners, they get very difficult to deal with later. Renew your commitment often.

Every healthy relationship has conflict. Avoiding conflict is not healthy. Don't make it your goal. Remember, your Mom-Who-Doesn't-Like-Conflict is saying this. When you hear the rock in the tire, you don't drive along hoping it'll just go away. You don't want the tire to go flat. The conflict is there, so you stop, inspect the tires, find the rock, remove it, and then check for damage. Did you hear that? *Check for damage.*

Sometimes conflicts are minor rocks in the tire. Pulling the rock out is the end of the story and you both go on. Other times damage has been done. Fixing the tire depends on how much damage has been done. More on this in Tune-up #4.

Speak the truth in love[2]. If you can't talk about something with her, then you *need* to talk. Letting it go will *not* make it go away. Give and receive permission to be honest with each other. Part of that honesty is permission to bring up the topic until it's resolved. Discuss it awhile, stop, and come back to it another day after you've both had time to reflect. You also need to have and give permission to be wrong. Napa lets you make mistakes in buying parts. Let the same rule work in your marriage.

God's mercy and love for you begin new every day.[3] That's your model for resolution commitment. When you allow conflict to build up, attitudes get very difficult to budge. Sometimes even penetrating fluids like tears have no effect. People get broken. Everyone has something to learn here. Just be certain that the replacement attitude or process has equal or greater strength than what you started with.

When applying new nuts and bolts to a vehicle, there's a sequence to follow and a specific amount of pressure or torque to use. If the pattern isn't followed, the component gets warped. The same is true with conflict. Too much pressure (control) or too little (apathy or passive/aggressive behavior) and the relationship gets warped. It takes a lot of time to tighten, test, check torque, loosen and re-tighten to get it right, but you do it because of your commitment to get it right. If you put in that kind of effort on a vehicle, learn to do the same for your marriage.

There are three C's to conflict, a sequence to loosen and tighten, if you will: *conflict, counsel, comfort.*

Conflict brings the problem into the open. It doesn't reveal all of the problem or even the real problem. Conflict is a dummy light letting you know you need to investigate further.

Then *counsel.* Teach each other what you mean, what you want, what you need, and how it needs to be presented.

Follow counsel with *comfort.* Conflict drives a wedge between partners because the value of the person and relationship are brought into question. Affirm, affirm, affirm.

When you were little, you had to be taught what I meant when I said, *"Listen to me."* Telling you to listen before you knew what that meant was pointless. You and your bride are new to each other. You have to start with the basics of telling each other what you mean, otherwise you'll have more conflicts. If neither of you knows what you mean when you say certain words, there are going to be misunderstandings. You're going to be training each other much longer than your parents did. Take time to do a good job.

Another tip from auto mechanics: When you take something apart, it should be done with care. Remember, a goal is to put parts back together properly. On a vehicle you keep track of the sequence in which parts are removed. Take the same care with a wife. Conflict often involves taking apart attitudes, feelings, or beliefs. Do so with great care.

It isn't always possible to put things back together once you start taking them apart, so plan ahead to give yourself the greatest chance of success. Organization helps. Write things down. Put all the little bits in a very safe place and dedicate yourself to sticking with the re-assembly until all the parts are back where they should be.

Technique #3: Commit to Goals.

You won't get anywhere if you don't have a destination. You don't get behind the wheel not knowing where you're going, or why, on a daily basis. If you know where you're going and why in your relationship, it's more likely you'll arrive there. Goals are not just a personal thing. Set them as a couple and as a family. Tune-up #2 covers setting goals in depth.

Commit to setting and communicating realistic goals for yourselves and your family. You'll have fewer conflicts if you practice this technique. If my mate sees my time as uncommitted, he's more apt to want my companionship and attention. If he knows I'm working on a project, what my deadlines are, and why I'm committed, he gives support by not asking for more of my time. It's all in communication.

Technique #4: Commit to Values.

GPS systems are handy because there's always more than one way of getting somewhere. Everyone has different values. It isn't a matter of who's right or wrong. If you try to change each other, you'll both end up unhappy. Learn to see her values as a strength in your relationship. She has a different route than you do, but she's working toward the same destination. There are GPS routes which support your values and those which delay you. Sometimes you need the direct route. Sometimes the leisurely pace is just fine. You need to know and support each other. Commitment to marriage means commitment to values and goals.

Technique #5: Commit to Communication.

We'd love it if we didn't have to slow down and communicate what we mean with others. It'd be handy if they "just knew" what we meant. Mind-reading is not one of the skills you can acquire. It takes time and commitment to understand and be understood. It takes commitment to outgrow selfishness and pride. It takes commitment to the marriage itself to do the hard work of getting along so you can reap the benefits. All communication is a skill. You practice, you get better. You don't practice, it stays difficult.

Know that men and women approach communication differently. Women are often taught to be nice. At some point being nice sacrifices honesty. Being nice attempts not to hurt feelings. Being nice can be very confusing. You may have to encourage her many times over that you want honesty from her more than you want nice. Learning to speak the truth in love[2] is a skill. I'll say it again: skills, if practiced, can be acquired. Commit to strengthening your marriage with honest communication.

Note: You may have to ask her more than once. Often the *last* thing she tells you is the most important. By then, you've stopped listening. This brings us back to the listening skills. You don't just start the engine, listen for a nanosecond and go away. That's listening for what you want to hear, not listening to hear what's really there.

The key is to learn to hear what she means, not what she says. You have to learn to use all the tools and all the techniques listed here. You use more than one tool and more than one technique on the car. Have the same expectation in maintaining the relationship with your wife.

And that brings us to the final part, **Working Facilities**.

There is a time and place for everything. Some guys drive up to the parts store, buy the goods and change the oil right there in the parking lot, leaving a mess for someone else to clean up. Routine maintenance and tune-ups can make a mess. Vehicle rides or evening walks are great for small jobs. Anything other than routine maintenance needs to be done in proper facilities. Take a weekend away to set goals. Go camping. Go hiking. Make it your kind of fun, but stay focused on the goal. Make sure you set aside enough time to disassemble, replace/repair, and clean up. Don't spend a few hours taking your relationship apart and then try to limp through the week without doing the rest of the steps to get it back in working order.

Think back to your dates again. The places you went on dates were all working facilities because you dedicated time, money, and effort in a context you enjoyed for the purpose of getting to know each other.

Note: In all this writing, I'm not trying to clone you into a me-model. The purpose of this book is to equip you to do *your* job. Take time to evaluate everything in this book. Compare it with your bride. Use what fits and set aside the rest until needed. Use your brain.

You're doing great. Keep going.

CHAPTER 6

Jump Starting
Or, Getting Chocolate Right

I FIND IT interesting that Jump Starting is under the Introduction in car manuals. It's basic to vehicle care because it happens. You fail to keep her warm enough for her environment and she refuses to start. You leave the lights on, you drain her dry. She goes until she drops and needs help to get going again. It happens to everybody. Jumping in the driver's seat, turning the key and yelling at her for that dead sound under the hood does no good.

There are specific steps for getting power back on for your wife.

1. Make sure her "ignition" switch is turned off. If she's down, she's down. You can't power her up on the run with a double shot latte.

2. Your wife carries loads which drain her. If she's burned out, do your best to remove those loads. You can't power her up while she's being drained. How? Call and cancel or revise her schedule with her help. Get a babysitter. Get someone to bake the cookies for school. If you don't have good communication, you won't know this stuff. If she's really burned out, or sick, she may not be in any shape to tell you. You have to know her well enough ahead of time, just as you have to know how to connect positive to positive and negative to negative in order to jump the battery. The risk of getting it wrong can be explosive.

3. Shield your eyes. Remember, when power is lost, she's touchy and

likely to blow up if not handled correctly. Love covers a multitude of touchiness.[1]

4. Take care as you power her back up. Let her idle a bit. Let her have time and space to re-charge. It takes three times as long to recover from burn-out than it does to take care against getting there in the first place.

Dead batteries tend to occur at inopportune moments. Guys, you have no idea how low she's getting most of the time. To know, ask. Just as you can't tell by looking at a battery if it's dead or not, you can't tell by looking at her if she's about to lose power. Her blood pressure goes up when she comes home after work. Yours goes down.

For most guys, coming home means relaxing. For her it means laundry, cooking, children, and getting ready for work the next day. And then you twinkle at her and get all miffed when she says no. She's pooped! Tell her you'll take the kids while she goes and gets new shoes, new clothes, or her feet done at the spa. Check her Authorized Parts list. Sometimes she just needs five minutes without any demands on her. If you're not going to cook dinner, then set the table, haul out the trash, or do the dishes—anything to lighten the load you expect her to carry. Remember you're *partners* in this marriage stuff. If she can't carry her load, you have to do it until she's back up. Learn to check the battery more often so she doesn't lose power.

WARNING: Do _not_ call taking care of your own children babysitting. You babysit other people's children; you take care of your own.

Most guys assume that flowers and candy do the trick. If your wife's battery is dead, they won't. She needs new life, not polish. The exception is chocolate. Chocolate is very tricky. If she's feeling fat she wants chocolate, but if she's *really* feeling fat, she doesn't want to be an Indy lap near the stuff. You can't tell by looking at her. A dummy light helps. Get a refrigerator magnet (see Appendix II) that refers to chocolate. When you see the magnet on the fridge, the dummy light is glowing. It's time for you to immediately provide chocolate.

The other tricky part is that not all chocolate is created equal. There are favorites and there are definite no-goes. Get the list from *her*. Remember the dangers of dealing with batteries.

THE Factory Authorized Chocolate List

Betty Crocker/Duncan Hines mixes

Brownies

Cookies

Ghirardelli

Godiva

Hershey's

Hostess

Ice Cream

Lindor

Milkshakes

Nestle's

Oreos

See's

Toll House

Whitman's

Other

Hubby quote: *"It's worth investing in quality tools. Don't get the cheap stuff. If you use quality tools on a quality vehicle, it'll last you indefinitely."*

CHAPTER 7

Jacking and Towing
Or, "How's this gonna work if you don't do what I say?"
Kevin Costner, Open Range

A VERY GOOD question. How *is* this supposed to work? Jacking and towing are not the way to get somewhere, but they're occasionally necessary. Jacking and towing are meant to get you out of trouble, to a place of repair. Don't let it become a way of life. What fun is it to always be dragging her places?

Sometimes things go flat. You need to stop, get out of your normal relationship to her and give her a new footing. The goal is not to change the tire. If that were true, you'd sit beside the road after the tire was changed. The goal is to get back together and get moving again. Serving her in this manner is your leadership.

Note: Don't mistake her need of your aid as inferiority. There'll be times when your driving isn't so hot and she carries you where you're going. Her need for your help is evidence of her humanity, not gender weakness.

There are safety issues involved. After you've lifted her up, don't lose focus. You're there to change the tire. Don't start the engine. Don't work on the carburetor. *Change the tire*. Fix the flat. Stay focused. The flat may reveal other issues requiring attention, but beside the road in the gravel isn't the place to deal with them. (See Working Facilities)

Deal with the flat. Call for assistance, if necessary, and carry her to a place of repair. Know your own strengths and weaknesses. *"Make a careful exploration of who you are and the work you have been given, and then sink yourself into that. Don't be impressed with yourself. Don't compare yourself with others. Each of you must take responsibility for doing the creative best you can with your own life."*[1] You might want AAA to do all the work. You may want a towing company to haul the two of you to a garage. Or you may prefer to be hauled home and work on things together in your own shop. There's no right or wrong way here. Choose what suits the two of you.

Changing a tire is a simple procedure, but not without some risks. Sharp edges, normally covered, get exposed. Be wise. Save your critical comments for yourself. You might need forgiveness later in the day.[2]

Note: Vehicles tend to roll away from you (or crush you) when you're lifting them up for repair. Set the parking brake.

Make sure the jack and spare are in good enough shape to carry you through any emergency. If you don't like lying on rocks or in snow while you're changing a tire, then pack a tarp, space blanket, or something. Don't like dirty hands? Pack some gloves. The point is, don't refuse to take responsibility for this aspect of vehicle/wife maintenance then act as though you're a victim of some severe trial. It's part of routine maintenance to make sure the safety equipment is functional and that you'll be comfortable using it.

Towing

This brings up the issue of your role as leader. A touchy subject in this day and age. Women are afraid of and downright resistant to following, and men are politically-corrected out of doing anything for fear of attack. Leadership needs to happen. Where there are only two with no third voice to break up tie votes, an agreed-upon order must exist.[3] Men make mistakes in leadership. So do women. The fact that we make mistakes doesn't justify changing the roles. Men become better leaders when they have both the responsibility of leadership, *and* make mistakes. They burn through a set of tires laying rubber and have to pay for a new set, learning that such behavior, while fun, costs them four new tires.

We all suffer the consequences of our mistakes. There were times when I refused to follow and went my own way. Sometimes it was a mistake. Sometimes it wasn't a mistake, but it still eroded the relationship, so it still wasn't fruitful. *It isn't as simple as being right.*

If I'm going to be responsible for myself, then I can't demand he be on call 24/7 to rescue me. Marriage is not a magic-genie-bottle relationship. If I'm going to expect him to rescue me from my mistakes, he has a right to tell me when I go beyond his ability or willingness to put himself at risk. I have the same right. If he wants to entertain and expects me to do the cooking, then he needs to check with me before inviting everyone over. Ladies, if we're going to expect them to *lead* the family, then we have to let them be the head of the family. If I have responsibility for something, I need authority over it as well. If I don't have authority, then I can't take responsibility. Leaders who have no authority aren't leaders.

I appreciate one pastor who said he has never seen a following problem that wasn't directly related to a leadership problem. Following doesn't mean chucking your brain, individuality, opinions, gifts, or talents. *God wants us to use our intelligence, to seek to understand as well as we can.*[4] But if you expect to be married *and* have it all your way, why did you marry in the first place? Marriage is two coming together as one, not two independent parallel units.

Likewise, leadership doesn't mean dictatorship, benevolent or otherwise. Leadership implies a group going in a specific direction. It implies common values and goals. You and your wife have marriage values and goals. Know what they are. Know where your marriage is going. Then take responsibility and lead it there. Leadership is meant to get everyone "there," with all members in good shape, feeling a sense of accomplishment. In order to do that, the leader must recognize and put to use individual strengths of each member.

WARNING: Don't get used to either towing or jacking. That isn't the marriage you want. Always towing her around means you're not fixing what's broken. Flat times in your relationship can happen to anyone. Checking the tires frequently helps eliminate being worn down, out of balance, or needing a bit of rotation. The goal is to get back together, going the same direction.

When my husband and I were dating he asked me to please let him open doors for me. *"It'll help remind me to show respect for you."* I'll sit still for that.

This role stuff is tricky. It's a blend of culture, family, personality, and whatever. At its base must be mutual respect. Domination is an easy way to look good in front of others. It's often a symptom of lack of courage.[5] Instead, live *free from the stifling atmosphere of pleasing others and fitting into the little patterns that they dictate.* [6]

Being named Head of Household can be very heady unless you remember it's not about you. It is about your leadership. *Each of you must take responsibility for doing the creative best you can with your own life.* [7] Dominating others is not a creative gift. Leadership is. Learn the difference.

I appreciate my husband because he told me I have the right to expect him to grow spiritually. Why? I'm supposed to follow him. It's that open-the-door thing. In order for him to lead well, he has to be growing. He asks me to hold him accountable. I don't lord it over him and he doesn't lord it over me.

We have a construction business. Construction tends to come with bad language. He asked me to help him in this area. We agreed on his using two bad words a month. He found that having permission to fail gave him confidence. If I'd said the tolerable level was zero, he would have given up. Being given permission to fail encouraged him to try harder. It works. I respect him for the ways he tries to honor me, even when he fails.

Leadership means *mutually* submitting to one another.[8] You seek the best for her daily, she seeks the best for you daily. Don't try to make her into a guy. If you like femininity, then your leadership has to encourage her to buy and participate in the stuff that yields femininity. If she likes masculinity, then she has to support activities which help you be the strong protector she likes. Just make sure those independent activities don't take away from the two of you.

There are safe places to support her and there are places where, if you try to give her a lift, you'll end up breaking her instead. She has natural strength. You have to work with *her* strength, not what is most convenient for you. She'll resist if you try to pull the weight of your relationship by yanking on the bumper instead of connecting to the frame. If she isn't following, check your connection. Pushing the car is not fun. Neither is pushing your wife.

Safety is a major consideration when towing. That's why you attach a safety strap. Remember those wedding vows? For better *or* for worse? The vows, made not only to each other, but also to God, are a safety system. The unexpected happens at the most inopportune times. Be a man of your word.

I remember one time I got the call. "*The truck's down. Come and get me.*" I packed up two small boys. The school program was due to start and one of the boys was a lead frog. We raced down the road to the stranded vehicle. It was agreed that I would tow and he would steer the non-functional truck. It's never as simple as it sounds. We were on country roads—there were no shoulders, just curves and hills—miles of them. I would just get the hang of keeping the tow rope taunt and the road would change. Jerk, pull, yank. Jerk, pull, yank. It went on for miles. We stopped and I received instruction to quit yanking. Like I wasn't trying to begin with. I tried again. The star frog beside me started singing, "*YANK-ee Doodle went to TOWN, RIDE-ing on a PO-ny.*" His little emphasis matched the jerking and pulling as I struggled to find balance. I told the little frog to be quiet. All the jerking and pulling made the trip a slow one. We passed the school and people were waiting out front for the frog. Great. We got home and yelled at the frog to hurry up. The frog ran and fell on the door. Now the late front-and-center frog had a goose egg. It really is important to get towing right.

Towing isn't the same for every model. Manual transmissions handle differently than automatics. Your wife model requires leadership suited to *her* style. If you can adjust leadership for your vehicle based on its need, then you can adjust leadership for your wife based on her need. How do you know whether she's automatic or manual? Ask her. Simply asking, *"How do I do this?"* works. The best information comes from reviewing a time when she needed you in the past. Ask her what worked and what didn't. Ask her what's important to remember the next time. *Write* her answers below. Remember to look for *her* characteristics instead of defaulting to your way of doing things.

1.

2.

3.

4.

5.

JACKING

1. Choose a level surface. Ask, *"Are you ok with this?"*

2. Block the wheels so she doesn't walk away during this change. Ask her how you can help her hang in there until the change is complete. This is meant to be just a tire change, not a major event.

3. Turn on the hazard flashers. Get her out of the flow of life until it's done. Ask her, *"Who can I call, what needs to be canceled or moved?"*

4. Set the gear in Park. Eliminate phone calls, pagers, e-mails, etc. until she says she's ready for them again. Use wisdom. She may try to keep rolling along.

TOWING

1. Adjust your expectations. Don't expect to go swiftly (in excess of 25 mph) nor far (over 15 miles) while towing. If she requires towing, don't expect business as usual.

2. Release the parking brake. Take care of whatever makes her dig her heels against this process. What is she worried about, afraid of? You don't have to do it all yourself; find someone to help. Towing equipment is specifically designed for your model. Don't tie a rope on the bumper and start hiking. Remember the star frog.

3. Put the gear in Neutral. While you're moving to a place of repair isn't the time to discuss the future nor put it in reverse and hash over the past.

4. Unlock the steering. She is fully capable of taking off without you in the driver's seat. And you have no business sitting behind the wheel trying to steer her while she is being towed. Let go.

5. Power steering and power brakes don't work when the power is off. Don't expect power from her. No criticism over why she needs towing. Save it for a tune-up.

CHAPTER 8

Automotive Chemicals and Lubricants
Or, Beyond the Three C's: Cards, Candy and Cubic Zirconium

GUYS EXPECT FLOWERS, perfume or candy to do the trick every time. That makes as much sense as putting transmission fluid in the brake system. Different parts of your wife's make-up require different chemicals and lubricants. There are *twenty-seven* different chemicals and lubricants listed in my vehicle manual. You must move beyond flowers, candy, and cards to care for your wife.

Cleaners: These are used during downtime to work on specific systems: brakes, carburetor, electrical. They dissolve what builds up in a normal relationship. In order to know which one to use, you have to know which system you're working on. Carburetor cleaner leaves a film and isn't okay to use on electrical parts. Cleaners aren't necessary for the daily operation of your relationship. Cleaners are explained in Maintenance and Tune-ups.

Lubricants: There are ten different lubricants listed in my auto manual. Top of the list is motor oil. Top of her list is romance. Don't underestimate it. It rates as highly with her as sex does with you. Think of the rows and rows of oil types available at the parts store. Lots of different kinds out there, eh? And—you don't apply a little oil when you want to go somewhere and then leave her dry the rest of the time. Romance is unique to your wife, but once you learn her preferences, she's fairly predictable. I hear the groans out there, but it really isn't that hard. You already know what it takes because you aced it when you were courting. You spoke her language. You rang her bell. Ask her to tell you what was most important to her during your courtship. It never hurts to re-tell your love story. Tell her what attracted you to her. She needs to know what she did right as well.

Note: Romance is admittedly a little vague. One day candy and flowers fit, the next day they don't. Look at it this way: if she cooked the same food for you every day, even though it was your favorite, you'd get tired of it. The same principle applies to romance. When you run her a quart low all the time, pretty soon it'll take more than just oil. You'll have to change *all* the oil, *and* the filter, *and* check for damage to the engine.

Sometimes you'll get rid of all the past romance and start fresh. You can only get so much mileage out of one quart of oil and one episode of flowers. Don't plan on being so proud of yourself that you think your romance package will suffice for months and months. You wouldn't apply the same reasoning to sex, would you?

So how do you figure out romance? Start with *The Five Love Languages* by Gary Chapman. This book is as crucial to understanding your wife as her personality, goals, and values. Read it with her. This is a truck-talk book. Discuss it with her. Write down her preferences. Take time. The right oil is critical to the smooth running of your relationship.

LOVE LANGUAGES

HIS	List in order of preference	HERS
	Acts of Service	
	Gifts	
	Quality Time	
	Touch	
	Words of Affirmation	

If her primary love language is touch and she still isn't responding, then go to her secondary language and speak that to her. Keep going down the list until she's running smoothly. Most of her operational time is under the hood, out of sight. You're not inadequate because you don't innately know everything about her. Knowledge is different from understanding. You can know your wife well, but you'll never fully understand her. Adjust your marriage goal accordingly. If your goal is to understand her, you'll get frustrated every time you don't. You don't have to understand the physics which make your car run, but you can know your car well. Know your wife well. This is important stuff you'll use in later tune-ups.

Note: Sometimes you change the type of oil because the engine is under load: pulling hard or in cold weather. You have to pay attention to the level *all* the time and not let it get too low. You have to have a filter in place *all* the time as well.

Sealants: Ah—this is so easy. Listen.

"RTV Sealant *is one of the most widely used gasket compounds. Made from silicone, RTV is air curing, it seals, bonds, waterproofs, fills surface irregularities, remains flexible, doesn't shrink, is relatively easy to remove, and is used as a supplementary sealer with almost all low and medium temperature gaskets.*"[1]

Sealant is the equivalent of love. "*Love is patient, love is kind. It does not envy, it does not boast, it is not proud. It is not rude, it is not self-seeking, it is not easily angered, it keeps no record of wrongs. Love does not delight in evil but rejoices with the truth. It always protects, always trusts, always hopes, always perseveres. Love never fails.*"[2]

You aren't capable of this kind of love, but this love seals you together. It's why you make God part of your marriage. He *is* capable of it and *He* brings it to your relationship to achieve what you can't. If love alone sealed us together, there would be no divorce. Human love alone fails. Human love combined with God's love succeeds more often than not.

Chemicals:

Anti-seize compound. Great stuff! Seizing up gets back to the leading/following issue. Fortunately, there are signals that she is about to seize-up.

You need to be a student of your wife on this one. Not everyone gets quiet. One wife may lower her head and avoid eye contact. Another wife may jut her face forward and glare. Some wives get quiet; some get noisy. If you know the signals, you can avoid an entire lock-up of the system. What's lock-up? Digging in of her heels, rebelling, resisting, saying, "No" loudly or otherwise.

Note: Very often the simple act of stopping what you're doing slows down the seize-up process. Ask her what the problem is and lock-up begins to be avoided. *But*, you have to *really* listen to what she says, not just close your eyes until the sound stops, and continue forward.

CAUTION: If she has gone into silent mode and starts softly singing, "*God Will Take Care of You*," you're in big trouble. Pull off the road immediately and start diagnosing the trouble. Ask questions. Apply the appropriate cleaners and lubricants.

Anaerobic locking compounds come in medium and high strengths. Some parts of your relationship need more give and take. Other parts aren't meant to be messed with on a regular basis. Put them together and leave them alone. If you have to take the entire system apart, then be sure to use the same systems that locked you together in the first place: family, faith, and personal commitment.

"Oil additives…most oil manufacturers caution against using additives with their oils."[3] So does God. Romance is not the same as porn. Romance honors, respects, and enhances. Need a guideline? Sex is important enough to rate its own book in the Bible. Read *Song of Songs*, though probably not in the truck. God knew in the beginning that it wasn't good for man to be alone, and He knew why. He designed woman to complement that need. That doesn't mean woman is here as a beast of burden for man. God didn't create her that way. She came from man's side. We're meant to be beside each other, together, unified. Not one for the exclusive use by the other. Attitudes have a bad way of creeping in. Your job is to bring out the best in her.[4]

Gas additives on the other hand are positive options. They help dissolve stuff that builds up. Some additives even lubricate the engine. Additives are unique to your model. Ask her. One of my favorites that Hubby uses is, *"How can I help?"* He says I taught him that. I don't remember. I *do* remember how good it makes me feel when he says it!

Miscellaneous: This covers everything from brake fluid to wax and polish.

"Brake fluid is specially formulated hydraulic fluid that can withstand the heat and pressure encountered in brake systems."[5]

Knowing when to stop and how quickly to do so is a vital part of your relationship. In order to maintain her braking system, the two of you need honest communication. Braking is a safety issue. Squeals and softening of the system spell disaster. Honesty is the operational word here.

All this discussion about systems and fluids leads us away from an important point. All of your vehicle is not under a hood. There's an exterior needing regular washing and waxing, and an interior requiring regular cleaning of windows, vacuuming of upholstered surfaces, ArmorAll-ing of vinyl surfaces, and a regular cleaning out of the filing system—glove box, under the seats, in the side pockets.

She'll really shine if you go the extra mile on her wheels with a little Bleche White, some ArmorAll on her vinyl interiors, and do the labor of love of giving her a protective finish instead of the car wash squirt-on stuff. Don't forget my favorite, Rain-X, to help her see clearly during stormy weather. It's all little stuff. It takes time. It all yields great benefits.

How these products translate into your life depends on your model. ArmorAll might be praise for something she's done. Bleche White might be detailing her car, cleaning the fridge or oven. The thing all these products have in common is that they make her look *good*. Rain-X might be a purse, shoes, or having her nails done. It might be a class (tap dancing) or tools (paint brushes, paint and an easel). It'll vary, so get her input. Have fun. Watch her shine.

CHAPTER 9

Safety Or, Grounding, Goggles, and Ear Protection Or, Hold Still and It Won't Hurt

"REGARDLESS OF HOW enthusiastic you may be about getting on with the job at hand, take the time to ensure that your safety is not jeopardized. A moment's lack of attention can result in an accident, as can failure to observe certain simple safety precautions. The possibility of an accident will always exist, and the following points should not be considered a comprehensive list of all dangers."[1]

Essential DO's and DON'T's

DON'T default to your way! Remember—she isn't you.

DON'T start something, not finish it, then try to go again, ignoring the unfinished business.

DON'T try to force change. You'll bang your knuckles every time.

> DO write things down.

> DO take time to do it right the first time.

DON'T expect perfection—from yourself or from her.

> DO make allowances.

DON'T try to work on an overheated wife. Wait until she cools off.

DON'T try to touch an overheated wife.

DON'T let her toxic stuff remain on your skin. There's a difference between being responsible *for* and responsible *to* another person.

DON'T allow your spill-overs to remain or you'll slip on them. Once the work is over, clean up with some sort of celebration—going for a drive, an ice cream, a walk, a movie—whatever toots your horn.

> DO use the right tool for the right job.

> DO make sure the right tool is the right size. Using too much or too little of even the right thing will still get your knuckles skinned.

DON'T push. Always try to draw her toward you. This is not a physical thing—it's a love thing.

DON'T try to lift heavy problems alone. Get help.

DON'T rush or take unsafe shortcuts to finish a job.

DON'T include children in your overhauls. They need to see you two together—not tearing things apart.

> DO wear eye protection. Love covers a multitude of sins. How you look at her will influence how you treat her. Thoughts become words, words become actions, actions become character. Guard your heart and mind well. Better yet, ask God to help you guard it.

DON'T allow your stuff to get tangled in her moving parts. When she operates at her peak performance, it's a blessing to you, not a threat.

> DO make certain that any outside assistance you rely on is reliable. Cheap advice won't stick around to help you put the parts back together. Look for experience, success, and commitment when you enlist help. Some dude on the internet or at the water cooler isn't the right choice.

DO get someone to check on you periodically when working alone on a vehicle. Just because you're working alone and doing a good job of it, doesn't mean you don't need someone to check on you.

DO try to be logical.

DO keep the lubricants for your relationship out of the reach of children. Let children have a childhood. Don't burden them with the workings of marriage.

DO remember that your marriage affects the lives of those around you. Take good care of it for everybody's sake.

Asbestos

What you breathe in will either fill you with life or take it away. Friction produces dust and inhaled dust causes breathing problems, both with your vehicle and your relationship.

Not all friction is bad. Some friction is necessary for the smooth running of your relationship. But friction causes dust. Dust settles into small places and becomes a big problem. Insulating and sealing products are the very ones that, under regular use, produce the airborne stuff that, if not dealt with, will accumulate and take the life right out of your relationship. It's not so much *beware* as it is be *aware* of what is in the air between you. Again know the difference between being responsible *to* and responsible *for* others. Guard yourself from taking in what isn't meant for you.

Fire

"*They don't call it internal combustion for nothing.*"[2] The very thing that makes you scoot down the road and have a pleasant journey is also the very thing that can blow up in your face. *Spark. Fire.* The words conjure up excitement and pleasurable anticipation. They're meant to. But when that natural force gets out of hand, somebody gets burned. The remedy?

Keep the relationship well ventilated with open communication. Don't bring fire to the mix then act surprised when it blows up. If you regularly have fire coming out of your mouth, get a patch and stop smoking everyone around you!

CAUTION: Remember to take care of your own static-fire. What you allow to build up in you can spark to her and cause a blow-up. She's inert until you come home with your bad day built up and unload too near her. Discharge your own energy in a safe place so it doesn't spark to her or other innocent bystanders.

And—*It is strongly recommended that a fire extinguisher suitable for use on fuel and electrical fires be kept handy.*[3] If you're going to work on the systems of good relationship, then keep guidelines handy to prevent any discussion from getting out of control. Draw up your own list of fair-fighting rules. Agree to abide by them. Agree on how to handle it when somebody breaks the rules. Brainstorm as many situations as possible so your extinguisher works well. Then be certain to check the charge on your extinguisher regularly. Do the rules still work? Do we need to modify, change, add or subtract anything?

FAIR FIGHTING RULES

No swear words, yelling or sarcasm

Be honest

Stick to the topic at hand. Agree to come back to other topics later

No comparing

No going to bed mad

Make sure your goal is to get the relationship back on track – not to be right

Be a problem solver, not a people changer

DATE:

WHEN WE MESS UP WE'LL

Ask forgiveness

Give forgiveness

Be honest

Make amends

Confess

Do better

Date:

AFTER CONFLICT RESOLUTION WE'LL

Build a positive memory

Not use the conflict as a weapon in future engagements

Review the definition of love in Chapter 2

Review our Marriage and Personal Goals

Date:

Fumes - Certain fumes are highly toxic and can quickly cause unconsciousness or even death...4

The stuff that comes out of your mouth can be highly toxic to those around you. The *way* you say things can be toxic even if the words aren't. Remember this is a customized manual. Get feedback from *her* about the way your language affects her. Give her feedback about her fumes—the looks, the tone of voice. You both have to understand how you impact each other, and you won't know unless you take time to tell each other.

We're talking about relationship fumes here. Obviously smelling good is important, even after you get married, if you want a quality relationship. If she loves some scent, then wear it! It's a lot cheaper and less time consuming than counseling! It may even be one of those romance points. Just don't try to use it to replace taking a shower.

While we're on the subject of points, you can get a few extra by washing your own smelly, stinky stuff once in a while if you don't usually do the laundry. It's no fun handling week-old sweat. You see it as part of the trophy after winning the city league. She sees it as smelly stuff. <u>*Your*</u> smelly stuff. In her head she might be making a transaction and you'll possibly owe her. At some future date, she'll expect you to clean up after her uncomplainingly and without thought to *your* schedule.

Smells leave powerful memories. As infants some of our earliest memories are of smells. Ask if she likes the shampoo, the soap, the deodorant. If she doesn't, find something new. Flowers, candy, candlelight, music and dancing can all be rendered useless if BO or the wrong fragrance knocks her over.

The Battery

Batteries, like gasoline, are highly combustible. The difference is that the energy is stored, whereas fuel energy is meant to be consumed. The stress of long, cold times drains her battery. In extremely cold times, you may need to apply an outside source of heat to keep her from drying up. The battery and fuel are so important they need to be checked every time you go somewhere. Don't take her for granted. Don't stop paying attention. Make sure she's able to store enough energy to carry her through her day.

Household Current

When using power from outside your own relationship, make certain it's solidly grounded and not bringing a spark or short to your operating system. Friends are great but a huge red flag goes up when you start telling a friend what you ought to be telling each other. If you catch yourself saying, "*I've never told her this*," then you need to solve that problem immediately. The dummy light is in the danger zone. *Why* haven't you told her? If you're telling others, then you're passively telling her without taking the responsibility. The secret is out once you've told the friend and it may get back to her. Our need for friends is important, but don't let them take the place of honesty in your relationship at home.

Secondary Ignition System Voltage

We're not safe to love another person until we love God. What's at risk is transactional love. You make a transaction, giving with the purpose of getting; I'll love you *if* you'll love me. All such love is bound not to hold up because we simply can't promise to always love another person. We're human. We won't love always and forever, no matter which love songs we prefer. Again we come to that concept of goals. If the "*I do*" at the marriage was a commitment to another person alone, the union is automatically weak. We're emotional creatures. In emotional states we make poor decisions. If our vows were made to God *and* to the other person then at least one-third of the union will always be in His right mind and available to get the mess sorted out. As inevitably as tires wear out there will be messes. It isn't a matter of *if* but of *when*. Plan for them.

One of God's functions in your marriage is filling you up with His love so you don't demand love from your mate that she can't give you and you can't give her. "*Love never fails.*"[5] is about God's love, not human love. Human beings don't love the same way God does. When we know we're loved by God absolutely, then we aren't trying to get someone else to love us absolutely. We're free to enjoy what we each *can* give instead of always pecking for what we can't.

NOTE: CAUTION: WARNING: Trying to mess with this system while her engine is running or turning over could prove fatal to the relationship. You *both* have to stop in order to work on the relationship.

You're doing great. Hang in there.

CHAPTER 10

Conversion Factors
Or, I Did Too Tell You

LET'S FACE IT. Men and women don't speak the same language. They don't even think the same way. A wonderful book to read—together—is *Men Are Like Waffles, Women Are Like Spaghetti* (Bill and Pam Farrel). Men's thoughts go from one box of the waffle to the next box. He has a specific box for mowing the lawn and when he's in it, he's thinking about mowing the lawn. Period. Women's thoughts are more like a plate of spaghetti. While she's talking on the phone, she can also be cooking, doing laundry, feeding a small one, and planning a party. This difference has nothing to do with intelligence or thinking patterns.

Men can think in abstract/random ways, and women can think in concrete/ sequential patterns. While they're thinking great thoughts, however, men do so from a box and women do so from a plate piled high. Women are like wiring in the vehicle. Her wiring is connected front to back, side to side, inside and outside *all at once*. Men are more like the individual components.

Note: Abstract/random and concrete/sequential patterns of thinking aren't the domain of one gender. If you really liked the personality testing, look up this type of testing to see where the two of you fit. It's customizing your tool box. See Appendix III.

Women think about many things at once, hence the wiring/noodle arrangement. Even though women may not follow a linear sequence of thoughts, they still come up with the "right" answer, but can't necessarily tell you how they got there. Sometimes they can tell you, but it leaves you dizzy. You should ask her at least once to tell you how she got an answer. You need to know how complex the noodle system is, even if you'll never personally use or understand it. You may even be able to convert some of her noodle answers into your waffle language. Hang in there.

A man will ask a simple question like, "*Did you balance the checkbook?*" He expects a simple answer. "*Yes*" or "*No*" would do just fine. What he gets is more like:

"*That bill from Desmon's hasn't come in yet and Fleur hasn't cashed the check we gave her. I did put my paycheck in last night. Oh, don't forget we have that insurance payment coming up in two months. But all the rest of the bills are paid.*"

He wonders, "*What does all this mean?*" In order to answer the question, a woman relays all the information listed on all the wiring touching the checkbook wire. To her, the answer isn't complete without all that information. The answer is obvious—she couldn't tell you which checks were outstanding and which weren't if she hadn't balanced the checkbook. She's giving you the *results* of balancing the checkbook.

You can press a more direct answer out of her, but it'll probably frustrate her unless you tell her you need a waffle answer instead of a noodle answer. She also needs to tell you when she just has to noodle.

When a woman starts talking, the man goes to his problem-solving box and listens for the problem he's supposed to solve. When he doesn't hear a problem, he tries to fit the conversation into another box or simply zones out. Your wife helps by telling you at the beginning, "*I just need to talk this out. I need a listener.*" You go to the listening box instead of the problem-solving box and both are happier.

Women don't purposely remember everything men have ever done, with some evil intent of one-upsmanship. It's just that they operate from a nest *full* of wires. Events are always connected to other events in our memory banks. Guys, on the other hand, have to go to the exact component where that memory is stored before they can remember all the incidents a woman brings up.

However, every experience does influence the man—sort of like a Belgian waffle instead of a regular one. His experience caused him to build a higher wall on that particular box. His behavior changes, reflecting his experience; he'll just have more difficulty knowing why.

Another necessary Conversion Factor for you to remember is personality. If she's not a clone of you, she's different. She'll think differently, reason differently, and come to different conclusions. Every man does what is right in his own eyes. Remember that. You're thinking she's illogical but what she's doing makes sense to her. A good question to ask when you don't understand is, *"How is this logical to you? Why is this right?"* Much better than *"That's a dumb thing to do! Why'd ya do that?"*

Note: If you ask her to tell you, then be prepared for a wiring answer.

Learn to value her personality and subsequent way of looking at life as strength rather than something that needs to be proved wrong or changed. With two points of view in the house you can anticipate more pitfalls and avoid them as you journey this road of life.

Think about the t-shirts you wear. Guys are living billboards for the products they use. Women aren't. You'll never see a woman wearing a shirt with Frigidaire, Maytag, or GE emblazoned on it. We won't wear baseball caps with Hoover, DustBuster, or SubZero. Every time you wear your Chevy, DeWalt, or Stihl apparel, remember *she's not like you*.

Example: Say you want to buy a house. You're the bottom line personality and have it all scoped out. It works financially, therefore it's a good decision. She disagrees. The financial package makes sense, but she's concerned about people. She sees the move as bad because the new neighborhood is in a bad area of town. She sees a weakness because she looks at it differently. The two of you then balance that new insight to make a joint decision.

Next we come to **The Point System.**

I'm not sure how to describe it, frankly. I think it's an embedded chip from the moment of chromosomal gender identity. It goes along with the wiring/noodles. It's more complex than any accounting system, because while you get points for what you do and lose points for what you do, or don't do, the points also go to other accounts and accrue interest. There are negative balance accounts and positive ones, sort of Accounts Receivable and Accounts Payable. Deposits are made by her friends, co-workers, and family. Deposits are given by people in stores or on the street. The clerk at the store where you buy the flowers thinks she has a pretty sweet guy. The clerk selling cards is impressed when she realizes you're buying cards and aren't even in trouble.

It sounds numeric, but there aren't any real numbers in this system. It's more like the gas gauge. You never know exactly how many gallons you have left, you just know you're full, half, or empty. It's the same with the engine temperature. The gauge tells you Hot or Cold. It doesn't give you degrees Fahrenheit. You don't need digits to tell you useful information. So how do you know how your points are stacking up? Ask. Sometimes just asking will get you a few points. *"How are my points doing? Did I get a lot of points for that or a few? Did I lose a lot of points for that or a few? I think I blew some points—how can I get more back?"* Again think of gas gauges. Some of them read full and then plummet. Others read empty for a long, long time. Learn your wife's gauge.

Like accounting, you have to set up your own books. There are some common headings and general categories. There are categories specific to your model. You have to communicate with her to find them out. A good way to discover your personal categories is to ask her what you've done that earned you points during courtship. Then ask her what you did during courtship that lost you points. I keep referring you back to your own courtship story because it's a goldmine of information for you. It's also the opening of your account in the point system. Since it's safely back in your history, you can discuss what went right or wrong more easily. Love has covered a multitude of those sins. Or not. You need to know.

POINTS

WINNERS	LOSERS

Plus points go into a daily score, a cumulative positive, and a negative score—rather like a P&L, Accounts Receivable, and Accounts Payable. Accounts Payable is a negative score. A single negative event point can get put in your daily score, the cumulative score, *and* your Accounts Payable score.

I hear grumbling and stereotypes out there. I hear the ram's horn call to retreat to the caves! Tell me you don't keep score. Guys keep score, but they do it with sports. They keep a mental count of averages, best years, best times, best scores. They also remember, just like women do, the times they've been hurt. They remember good times. It's all just boxed away in one of the less operational, not-easy-to-get-to component waffle boxes.

Points are sort of like your Man Bank. The difference is *you* keep track of your Man Bank balance and *she* keeps track of your points.

To men, the marriage is defined more in light of protection and provision. If the family is safe and provided for, then the score is positive. Women keep stats because they're nurturers and therefore more focused on relationships. We tell if relationships are okay by looking at how we're treated and how you treat others. Hence the long memory of who did what to whom when. Again—use this trait as a strength rather than resenting her on-board computer for what it tells you.

The nurturing nature of women is an indicator of the health of the relationship. When she's not nurturing because she's too stressed, that's a dummy light for you. Remember, dummy lights are there to raise the alarm, not defend a point of view or fix the problem. I'm not saying women have no responsibility here. I'm saying when the light goes on, it's time for both of you to stop and investigate. She may not know exactly what's wrong; she just knows something is.

No discussion of Conversion Factors would be complete without a bit of vocabulary. Remember the discussion of the Listening Tool? Vocabulary is where your listening technique comes into vital play. If you hear the following words, screech to a halt and get more information. These are dummy lights signaling impending disaster. The following is by no means an exhaustive list—just a few critical words you must know. Have her add her own words, if needed.

Fine: DEFCON Level 4

Uttered by a female, *Fine* means anything but the Webster's definition. Webster was a man—he just didn't know. *Fine* defies the noun/verb parts of speech. *Fine* is a sermon. It's a paragraph. A synonym of *Fine* is *Okay*. When *Okay* is combined with *Fine* as in, "*Okay. Fine.*" you'd better pull off the road and do some quick troubleshooting.

Fine means you've forced her to accept something she doesn't like, but she's through arguing. You aren't through with this subject, however. By forcing your point of view on her, you've told her that you two are in a battle to win, so she'll ponder until she finds a way to win as well. It'll likely take you by surprise as having no relation, in your mind, to the discussion which produced the *Fine* in the first place.

Once upon a time Grandma wanted Grandpa to stop and buy her an ice cream cone. Grandpa refused. She quietly accepted the *no* and later on went out and bought a skirt. I doubt he ever saw the connection.

"*Okay. Fine. You win!*" is the strongest version. This is where you lose audio and an entire conversation ensues in her head. You don't want to know what she's thinking. But you'll find out eventually.

Yes, dear: DEFCON Level 1-4

This is a corollary to *Fine*, but not as strong, unless she's yelling it. *Yes, dear* may mean she's ignoring you. It's equal is your *uh-huh* when you want to appear to be listening but really aren't. *Yes, dear* is not evidence of having a conversation. It simply means you're speaking and she's present. She's not giving you agreement. She's being your companion. You may be beating a dead horse with your conversation. She may be worrying about something else. The same things go on with you when you don't really listen to her. Change the subject. Better still, ask her what's on her mind and let her talk for a while. Find out what the *Yes, dear* means.

Sex

You were wondering when Mom would get to the important stuff, huh? Well, this is just vocabulary, not anatomy, so sit tight. Almost any statement I make here is bound to be contradicted by individual experiences. Remember how we began this section? There are too many makes and models out there for any one-size-fits-all statement to work. Besides that, you need to be a student of *your* wife's preferences, not The Average Woman's.

However, generally speaking, what men and women mean by "*sex*" is different. That doesn't mean they don't both like it. The conversion factor here is quite simple. When you say *sex*, she thinks romance. They aren't opposites. They're two sides of the same gasket. Romance to her yields good sex. When she's saying no or acting indifferent, don't retreat into your cave and have a pity party. Pour on the romance.

Knock off the groans and don't give me the *"It's too much trouble/I don't know how."* excuse. In the first place you *do* know how because whatever you did during courtship is what she likes. Too much trouble? That's what she thinks about sex without romance. That's why she loses interest. Sex without romance becomes all about what satisfies you and none about what satisfies her.

Romance *is* elusive, I'll admit. It isn't always expensive—a flower from the side of the road does the trick sometimes. Not everything you did during courtship was expensive, but it all had the purpose of showing you cared about her and thought about her. She still needs to know that.

Romance varies from model to model. Remember she isn't The Average Woman. She's your unique woman. This is where Factory Authorized Parts are required. She comes with bells and whistles—find out what they are. For further ideas attend the Womack conference at the Cannon Beach Christian Conference Center[1] on *The Song of Songs*. Or look until you find something that works for both of you. Ask her. Find out *why* she likes certain chick flicks.

NOTE: CAUTION: WARNING: *Love* doesn't mean sex, Intimacy doesn't mean sex. She's not you. Get to know her vocabulary just as you had to learn the vocabulary of the vehicle.

I don't care: DEFCON Level 1-4

You know how you have to listen carefully to the engine to discern whether a sound is alarming or okay? Well, you *really* have to listen to tone of voice when she utters, *"I don't care."* She may mean she really doesn't care one way or another. She may say *"I don't care,"* but mean *"Okay. Fine."* Or, the really tricky one is when she says, *"I don't care,"* but means you're making a transaction with her. In this instance, she's saying, *"This time it's your turn; next time it'll be mine. I'll expect to have my way next time because you've already taken your turn. I get to decide when it's pay-back."* If you hear *"I don't care,"* it's a good idea to ask, *"Are we making a transaction here?"* Hubby and I have simplified things so he doesn't have to ask. He's a D personality (DISC®), which means he likes to make decisions. When I really don't care, I tell him, *"Go, D, go!"* He can pick the movie, restaurant, or direction without any fear of reprisals. Other times I'll tell him, *"I don't care this time."* That clues him in to the fact that we're making a transaction. It means whatever "it" is wouldn't be my choice, but I'm willing to go along for his sake. It's all about keeping communication open and clear.

Nothing: DEFCON Level 1-4

As in, *"What's wrong?"*

"Nothing."

Hmm, could be an electrical problem, a steering problem, or something else. To find out, you need to listen and ask. *Nothing* can be used in the place of *Fine.* Definitely a steering problem. See Troubleshooting. If the tone of voice hasn't been firm, *"Nothing"* means she wants you to ask her more questions and drag it out of her. This is an electrical problem—you're holding of one end of the wire and need to follow the wiring all the way back to uncover the source of the problem. Remember to take safety precautions for random discharges. Be certain you're well grounded.

Know that if you don't fix the problem it isn't going to go away, so set aside time to check it out. It may be a simple case of loose wiring. Tighten communication and you're back in business. Don't let the word throw you off. You can master this stuff.

CHAPTER 11

Troubleshooting
Or, Groveling Made Easy

IF YOU'RE READING this chapter, I assume you're in trouble and need a quick fix. Your goal is to get to your destination. You don't want to change plans. You want to keep going. That may not be possible. The flat tire alongside the road on the way to the airport may reveal problems with the axle, brakes, shocks, or wheels. That's the way life happens. You have to deal with it.

I'd love to write a guide which covered every possibility you might encounter during marriage. My auto manual has six pages of troubleshooting text, *no* pictures, and that's *just* the introduction.

Unfortunately, my little metaphor breaks down here—women are biological systems, not mechanical ones. Translation: no two are exactly alike, and they will exhibit different symptoms which respond to different treatments. Even when you discover something that works gloriously once, it might not work the next time.

Why not? Because the first time carries the punch of novelty—like octane boost. Also, as we age we change. You don't want her to be thrilled at age forty by the same things that revved her engine at fourteen. She's going to change. So will you. Plan for it.

I wish I could give you a guide that *always* got you back on the road with minimum down time. Vehicles aren't that easy. Neither are relationships.

But they're worth it. You didn't buy the car, ignore it, expect it to take care of itself, yet be available any time you wanted it. Don't do the same thing with your wife. You can't say, *"I work and provide for you. Expecting more is unreasonable."* That's like buying fuel for the car and expecting it to never need anything else. That's illogical *and* unreasonable. The car won't last and neither will the wife.

Note: Remember there's no such thing as The Average Woman. I keep harping on that, but it's so easy to forget. We want simple, quick, easy answers. We think we want One-Size-Fits-All, but we really don't. What we really want is "easy." To enjoy your relationship, you have to take care of it, and that takes effort.

It's a no-brainer we forget: if you're not growing together, then you're growing apart. Repeat that. Courtship was your way of growing together. You put a lot of time, money, and energy into it. You don't have to keep up courtship, but you do have to keep up the effort to stay close. You don't notice drifting apart until it's sometimes too late.

One time Aunt Connie and I were in a rowboat at the lake. It was a beautiful day, the lake calm. We pulled in the oars and settled in for sunbathing. Sometime later we were rudely awakened by a wave. Thunderclouds were building. We weren't in the same place anymore. We hadn't noticed. We didn't set an anchor. We were in potentially serious trouble. The same thing happens to your relationship if you don't anchor the relationship with daily care.

It's tempting to try to do as little as possible. Dumb-ing down the life around you may make life easier, but the result isn't as rewarding. Who wants a dumb life? Take everything I say and see if it fits the two of you. Tweak this and make it your own. Enjoy the process of building a rewarding life together.

A word about factory blems. None of us came out of the factory without a few blems. The quickest way around this problem is to acknowledge that your parents did the best they could with what was available, as did their parents before them, and so on. Even if you could affix blame, what good does it do at this stage of life? Any damage done is not going to be undone by that person. They already did their best. There are no factory recalls where you can send her back and get a new past for her. We tend to cycle our way through life. What wasn't dealt with as a child will come up in each decade of life for us to take another whack at. The more time you work at resolving your stuff, the fewer breakdowns you'll have. The more stuff you take care of before marriage, the more fun your marriage will be. Once you're married, you have to deal with the entire package, blems and all.

CAUTION: Just because we uncover a blem doesn't mean we can get it all factory new. Some problems you live with. That doesn't mean you don't talk about them. Your attitude may be something like, *"This is a problem. When it crops up, I'll own the fact that it bothers me when you do it. If there are consequences, they'll be faced. We won't ask each other to live in denial about our blems. Our strengths are meant to cover each other's weaknesses,*[1] *not to grind each other into the dirt. Where one of us goes, the other goes along, so there's no benefit of pushing the other one off track."*

Try to have realistic expectations. We want bad stuff to go away so much we often live in denial, making the mess worse. If something happened, then it happened. We can't live for years and years in a situation—good or bad—and expect it to have no lasting influence. Even if you work on old history from your teens, life happens. Other experiences and maturity give you a different perspective. Every decade of your life those old issues come out and wave their flags at you. You may take a quick pit stop, look over the history in light of ten more years of maturity and come to new conclusions and a little more health and freedom. The pit stop may also bring to light the need to drive over to the pit crew and replace a worn part with some after-market upgrade. You don't have to live with old history carved in stone. Let God transform you into a new person by changing the way you think.[2] Life really is ten percent event and ninety percent attitude. You change your life dramatically by changing your attitude. Choose to live life as a victor, not a victim.

Keep your eyes on the horizon—don't get distracted by the lines on the road just in front of you. Stay focused on your ultimate goal, and you won't drive all over the road. You can't drive looking in the rear view mirror, either. If you need to examine something behind you, pull off the road and do so. You can't go forward and backward at the same time.

Make this fun. Keep it simple and short. Every guy knows as much about vehicles as he wants to know. That level isn't right or wrong, good or bad. It's individual. That's why some guys change their own oil and others visit Oil Can Henry's. You'll have similar preferences with your wife's maintenance. You may start out having someone else take care of some of it and then grow into doing more and more of it yourself. It's easy to say that the more you personally do, the better the relationship is, but that isn't always true. Do your best and keep learning.

Note: Just because you don't like to deal with some aspect of the fuel system, doesn't negate its need for maintenance. If you want a short and sweet list, put everything else into the Must-Get-Help list. Either way, commit yourself to learning a few more maintenance skills and expand your comfort zone.

I worry that you'll look at this list and start wondering when it's going to be *your* turn. This looks like a lot of effort! What's the payback? The payback comes because she purrs. Together you hum down the road. The road is less bumpy. You stop for fewer repairs. This is supposed to be mutual. If you begin by showing her care, she'll most likely reciprocate by showing you more care.

Use this section as a diagnostic guide. In some cases the fix is simple. Other times I'll refer you to a specific chapter for further details. As with your vehicle, check for the most obvious cause first. If that doesn't work, look for other causes of your problem. Remember, some problems arise out of normal use. Nobody's to blame. It's just life. Don't see wear as proof of faulty handling, get feeling all guilty, and then become resentful of the need for repairs or maintenance.

CAUTION: Even when you're the lead mechanic, remember the difference between being responsible *for* her and responsible *to* her. Her work is her work and you can't do it for her. You also can't make her do her work until she's ready to. Working on your own stuff gives you more credibility as her mechanic.

Don't forget that you aren't in this maintenance program on your own. If you cooperate with God, He can change the way you interpret your history and turn trials and tragedies into strengths.[3] Prayers tend to coalesce around the idea of, *"Dear God, make it go away, make it not hurt me or those I love."* There's a great deal more power in learning to pray, *"Dear God, make me equal to the task You've set before me."* True, whether you're looking at stuff in the rear view mirror, or a hazard in the road in front of you.

Remember—this is a manual. You don't pick up your car manual, read it cover to cover, and try and do everything at once. The same holds true here. If you try and do every tune-up and maintenance task listed, and all at once, you'll become frustrated.

Troubleshooting manuals are divided into eight sections: engine, electrical, fuel, cooling, clutch, axles, brakes, and suspension/steering systems. Your wife has equivalent systems. Take a look at how the systems break and how they get fixed. You'll get an idea of what comprises her systems because they break and get fixed in a similar manner.

I'll go into detail on the engine, and then let you figure out the rest of the systems.

Finally, a word from Haynes: *"Remember, successful troubleshooting isn't a mysterious black art practiced only by professional mechanics. It's simply the result of the right knowledge combined with an intelligent systematic approach to a problem. Always use the process of elimination, starting with the simplest solution and working through to the most complex…Finally, always try to establish a clear idea why a problem has occurred and take steps to ensure that it doesn't happen again…If a particular fuse continues to blow, find out why—don't just replace one fuse after another. Remember, failure of a small component can often be indicative of potential failure or incorrect functioning of a more important component or system."*[4] That's what I've been tellin' ya. (underlines are mine)

Engine

Engines convert fuel into useful power. They miss, stall, lack power, backfire, diesel, ping, and knock. They make sounds you can correctly interpret. They have behavior you recognize and diagnose. The same is true with your wife. So the question is, what power does your wife have, what fuel does she need, and what does she sound like when her system isn't running properly?

Any one of the following makes your engine run rough or not at all. Don't tell me women are too complicated! So is this stuff! With engine problems you'd systematically go through the following to find your problem: filters, gaskets, intake manifold, belts, hoses, clamps, seals, plugs, air cleaner, fuel, carburetor, fuel pump, choke control (I love that one), and emission systems. That's *fourteen* attempts to solve *one* problem! That's a lot of tenacity for a hunk of metal.

I love this: *"Use a stethoscope…to listen for vacuum leaks while the engine is running. A hissing sound will be heard."* [5] If you pay attention to the early signs of problems, you actually have to listen carefully for hissing. If you don't pay attention, everyone within earshot can hear the hissing, mostly because it proceeds to screeching.

Just because there's erratic behavior, though, don't start tearing down the engine. Check the fuel and electrical systems. We stopped at a rest area one time. The car full of guys next to us had the hood raised and they were tearing into their engine. I asked you if you could fix it. *"Mom, if they're tearing apart their carburetor when it's just a spark issue, I can't help them."* You knew from listening what the problem was, you knew they were on the wrong track, that the fix was much simpler than they were making it. Use the same wisdom with your wife.

Check the carburetor and air filter. If your car can exhibit multiple symptoms for the same broken part, then allow your wife the same permission. Then and only then delve into the deeper issues of vacuum leaks, EGR valves, gaskets and cam shafts.

Symptom:

Engine will not rotate when attempting to start [6]

1. Some wives like the road to themselves early in the morning. Other

wives like the hustle and bustle of downtown traffic. Still others prefer late nights. She is what she is. If she's having trouble starting herself, then do a quick check on goals and values. It's amazing how dull life becomes when you have no personal stamp on what you do each day.

2. If her engine isn't engaged in neutral to begin with, she won't start well in the morning. She has to go to bed without all the worries of the day. Why isn't she getting enough sleep? Will a spa day fix it? Tai chi? Music? Does she need to let go of responsibilities so she can rest at night instead of just thinking horizontally with her eyes closed for six-and-a-half hours? Is she worried? Is she working at a job she loves? Life is too short for either of you to work at jobs you hate. What you do during the day should make you content at night.

3. Is her battery low?

   a. Is she a diesel with a glo-plug that needs to warm up first? I hate alarm clocks. I hate being awakened with lights coming on. The two combined make me *really* grumpy. If an alarm clock is absolutely necessary, the best one I've heard of is a coffee pot on a timer. Set it up as near the bedroom so you're awakened by the aroma of coffee and the burble of water. Get creative—what sounds make her smile? Duplicate them so you wake up grinning even though you're going to work.

   b. Hours of life spent in meaningful daily activity equal a life well spent. Batteries and wives aren't recharged just because you let them rest. Depressed people can rest a lot and never get re-charged. The quickest way to drain her batteries is by living a life that isn't rewarding to her. Remember it's *her* system. *She* has to value it or it drains her.

4. Check her wiring—is her support network healthy and functioning? It isn't your job to make it so, but sometimes we need outside observers to help us see what's missing. Women need to feel connected. If she's having trouble getting started, she may feel alone too often. Ask her. Encourage her. Listen to her. This is wiring—you can't solve the problem for her but you *can* help her solve it.

5. Check her starter motor—her goals and values. Is she living in the present or in the future? How do you tell? If she says things like, *"When my boss retires, it'll get better." "When she graduates, it'll get better."* That's living in the future, a future which may never arrive. Ask, *"What would it look like for you to wake up excited about your day?"* Does she know who she is and why she's here? Does she have a life purpose? Does she know why her life is important? Today? Now? It's vital for you to be part of her process if you expect to stay married.

Engine rotates but will not start[7]

There are three possibilities in this case. She wants to go—goals and values are in place, but something's blocking her energy.

1. Her Fuel. Is she running on empty? Easy fix—get her refueled. Please **Note**: You do not personally manufacture the fuel. You may take her to a place of re-fueling. You may read her gauge. You may pay for the fuel. Knowing what is and what isn't your responsibility is very important. *Don't try to make the fuel.* Even with a full tank, however, she can still have difficulty. Her fuel pump, injection system or carburetor all might be interfering with the delivery of the stuff she needs to make her go. Ask her diagnostic questions—see #5 above.

2. Excessive Moisture. Note the word "excessive." Few models come completely devoid of moisture. Moisture is necessary, much as you might not like it. It's like a good de-greaser or cleanser. Moisture gets rid of accumulated emotional gunk and lets fuel flow free again. Excessive moisture, however, demands a bit of downtime until she's vented. Hold her, let her cry; don't offer solutions—just listen.

CAUTION: She doesn't always want you to fix things. Sometimes the act of crying *is* actually re-fueling her to go back and conquer what's been threatening to conquer her. Her tears help her gain energy, focus, and determination. Go figure. If you try to fix, all her steam's wasted. She gets frustrated at not being able to discharge at her target. *You're* likely to get the discharge. Re-read the safety tips in Chapter 9

3. Spark. Fuel is useless unless there's spark to give it effectiveness. Spark and fuel have to be connected as well. How are her spark plugs? How's her wiring, her distributor? Find the disconnect. Set the gap in her spark plugs. Re-connect the parts and she'll be back on the road with you in no time.

Starter motor operates without rotating engine[8]

Don't you wish every time the engine didn't start it was something simple, like filling the gas tank or jumping the battery? When it isn't so simple, you have to see if wear and tear has caused brokenness. You may have to remove the working part—that perfectly good starter motor—and look around it to see why its energy isn't being transferred. Or you may need to remove access covers and inspect for wear. Either way, it's no quick fix, so plan to stick with it until the problem is diagnosed, solved and all the parts are back where they belong.

Engine hard to start when cold[9]

1. Check first for caffeine levels—coffee or chocolate.

2. Check her battery—her place of stored energy—goals and values. Do they need revision? This isn't your job to do—it's hers, but she may need you to ask. Your job isn't to make the electricity and store it for her. Your job is to check the levels and add the input she needs to do her job. You add water to a battery, not some complicated formula. You can refresh her with simple words. Your input might be asking, *"How can I help?"* It might be listening to her. You might need to share your values and goals and those for your marriage to see if she still supports them.

3. Next, check her electrical and fuel systems. She can have a full tank, a charged battery and a functional engine and still have difficulty going. The electrical and fuel systems have to carry all that potential from one source to a place where it all comes together. She isn't being difficult any more than the car is. This is definitely electrical—follow the wiring and figure out what's wrong. Remember, you don't have to see what's in the wires to get them connected. Don't try to understand everything

going on here. Just keep testing one connection after another until you find the one that's not working.

4. The last item to check is her choke control. Even the name makes you smile. I bet you didn't know she had one! It isn't what keeps her from choking you. It brings to mind someone in control of her tongue. When it sticks, it's usually closed, allowing too much fuel to get through. See if all her wires are connecting on her guilt list of all the things she's done wrong or failed at. Open her up with some sincere compliments. Tell her what you value about her and how her value has grown over your years together. Ask her what she's afraid of. Go into you listening box.

Engine hard to start when hot[10]

The only difference between hot and cold no-starts is that instead of a choke control you need to check her air filter. Fuel and electrical systems need to be checked, the same as above. By now I hope you're getting the idea that while problems may look dissimilar, there's a finite number of ways to diagnose them. A systematic progression often solves the problem.

Check her air filter. Just as the air we breathe has impurities, which our bodies filter out and remove, your wife has an air filter designed to remove the impurities around her. Impurities are all over out there—in conversations, reading and viewing material, songs, movies, and thoughts. When too much negative garbage builds up, heat builds up. Heat rises as we daily confront all the stuff we don't like but can't change. Her air filter is her faith. Check for clogs. See if she needs a fresh perspective. Remember that a fresh perspective for a Jag is different than one for an SUV.

CAUTION: Even armed with a manual and a full set of tools, you're not guaranteed success every time you work on your vehicle. The same is true with a wife. Guys who buy car manuals do so because they *believe* they can fix it. They believe they can learn how. If you're reading this manual, I'm assuming the same is true about your attitude toward your wife. Maintenance gets easier with practice.

Starter motor noisy or excessively rough in engagement[11]

She's up and going, but there's a lot of noise beyond the perfect purr. It may be a simple fix—tightening those fasteners that hold her start-up energy in place. Or it may mean she's working so hard that gear teeth are beginning to break. These are attitudes that transmit power from one compartment of life to another.

No matter how much we like to take things apart and focus on just one system, we don't operate well unless *all* systems are functioning. Grinding teeth, like grinding gears, isn't good. Adjustments need to be made. Ask.

Engine starts but stops immediately[12]

It's funny how many different symptoms there are and yet the fixes start with a few simple basic check points: wiring, fuel, and electrical systems. Men look at women as having an overwhelming array of symptoms and assume each symptom requires a totally different approach and fix. Not so. Obviously, an engine problem won't be fixed by rotating the tires. You have to have a rough idea of where the problem is before you begin fixing it. As you and your wife communicate, you'll learn the difference between her tires and her engine.

If she starts, but just can't keep going, check the fuel and electrical systems again. Check for loose wiring. If all that passes inspection, then we get into engine problems. The engine is capable of running, the spark and the fuel are getting to the right place at the right time, but something's still wrong.

Check her gaskets. She needs to have a cushion between her working parts. It needs to be seated and sealed. It needs to custom fit *her* working life. Gaskets need to be flexible enough to stay in place with the daily highs and lows. You don't check gaskets at the gas station on the run. This problem takes time. Schedule time or the leaks will only get worse.

Electrical

Every time there's some independent source of power, there has to be wiring, hoses, linkage, and/or belts to transfer that energy to another part of the vehicle. Anytime you work on a system, it has to be reconnected to the rest of the engine or all your work will be wasted. It's a great diagnostic tool—if you did the work and there isn't any change, then look at the connections.

Just like the engine, there's a list of places to check for electrical problems: wiring, distributor, starter motor, fuses, ignition switch, timing, spark plugs, coil, alternator, rotor, timing, thermostat, light bulbs, circuit board, dashboard, and battery. Just like the engine, the fix is found in a systematic process of testing the obvious before you plow into the serious. Again— here are *sixteen* things to check to solve one problem. If you're that patient with the vehicle be that persistent with your wife.

The easiest place to start is with the battery—does she have enough fluid in her system? Are her cables corroded with gunk? Fill her reserve of energy up, clean or replace her terminals and you're all set. Easy fix.

Is she blowing a fuse all the time? Find out what the problem is—don't just replace the fuse. Find a solution that fits both of you and try it for a while.

An example: she comes home and blows a fuse because you left the bathroom a mess. You grudgingly pick up the bathroom. That replaced the fuse. The next time you leave the bathroom a mess, she blows a fuse again. Don't keep replacing the fuse. Discuss expectations. Work out a new agreement about picking up after yourself. Find out if the fuse is shorting to a bathroom problem when the wiring is actually frayed on the windshield wipers. If you just replace the bathroom "fuse" and don't solve the short in her vision, she'll just short out on another issue. Remember, you're on the same team. If your actions drain her energy, neither of you operates at your full potential. Solving the issue gives greater power to both of you.

If the quick fix doesn't restore the relationship, you have to delve into the more complex areas of starter motors, alternators, and coils. But no matter how complex the problem is, the fix always involves communication. It may involve an issue between the two of you. It may involve communication with parents, children, co-workers, or friends. When communication breaks down, energy gets misdirected. Remember, not all issues are your fault, but you do have the responsibility to help get them fixed. If her issues aren't fixed, neither of you gets very far. You're a team.

Example: I was quiet and Hubby noticed so he asked instead of assuming I was mad at him. I told him I felt lonely. He asked more questions. He listened. He told me he understood. The Fix: one game of pinochle and a walk around the block. He re-charged my battery by understanding what I was feeling. He got an 'A' and lots of points.

Communication is covered in every chapter of this book, so keep reading.

Brakes

"Before assuming a brake problem exists, make sure the tires are in good condition and inflated properly, the front end alignment is correct and the vehicle isn't loaded with weight in an unequal manner."[13]

Before assuming a brake problem exists, it's wise to do just what Hubby did—take time to ask questions and listen before taking action.

How do you know if you have a brake problem? Noise is a great indicator. You can be traveling down the road just fine, but when it comes time to turn or stop, there goes that squeal. Keep in mind that brakes are safety equipment. Ignoring noise isn't a wise idea. If you ignore the noise you risk stepping on the pedal only to find it going to the floor without doing a thing.

Brake pedals can comply outwardly—you press on them and they go down—yet not meet your expectations, even in an emergency. Wives can do the same. She can comply outwardly, yet be unwilling to stop, slow down, or change direction safely.

Pay attention to noise. The fix may be as simple as adding fluid. Don't avoid checking it out because you're afraid of what you might find. You might have air or contamination in the lines of communication. You might have to replace the entire system. If it isn't working, then no amount of telling how great it used to work is going to do you any good. When it's time for change, you have to make the changes.

Another symptom of a brake problem is pulling to one side during braking. If you're going to lead, you have to be trustworthy. Find out what her fears are and discuss them.

One of my favorite fixes is driving backward while pressing on the brakes. If the brakes aren't working going forward, then maybe it's time to look in the rear view mirror and go backward for a bit until the brakes have time to self-adjust. Some models require time to adjust to changes. If that's who she is, then you have to accept her style. She's not being slow to accept change because she's stubborn. Backing up won't hurt you.

Axles

Axles are funny things. They can break and you won't notice. Oh, you can hear a clunk, but if you keep driving, they keep working. I heard the clunk in Reno, drove three hours back to Grandma's and then another hour back to town to have the problem checked out. I was blessed. Driving highway speeds with a broken axle isn't recommended.

Neither is expecting your wife to keep going when she's broken. If you hear a clunk, click, knock, or road noise, stop and check things out. Keep in mind there's a front axle and a rear axle. You can't just check part of the system and expect everything you don't check to be okay.

The most important tool required is listening. Listen to the noise and hear *what* it tells you. Keep listening until you discover the *cause* of the noise. The fix may be as simple as adding fluid. Yes, you're working on complex systems in your relationship, but that doesn't mean all the fixes have to be done by a professional. See if fluid eliminates the noise. Refer to her custom list of lubricants you made earlier to find the right fluid.

CAUTION: Axles are responsible for carrying the weight of the relationship, for distributing the power of the relationship equally to four separate points of contact with the outside world. They all have to go in the same direction at the same time and at the same speed.

How do you know when you have a problem? How about if she won't go forward or backward? If shifting gears is rough or noisy, then you have a problem. How serious? Try checking the fluid and filters. If that doesn't work, then you may need to get professional help.

Suspension and Steering Systems

Suspension and steering systems make the ride smooth, safe, and help you easily change directions. When they break, the ride continues, but feels rough, or there's energy being spent, but you don't end up where you want to go.

The symptoms may look the same as brake problems. She may pull to one side or resist direction. She may act like the brakes and outwardly comply, but nothing happens when you turn the steering wheel. The difference is that clutches, tires, shocks, bearing and belts are *always* wearing out. If they're being used properly, they wear out. If they're used improperly, they wear out faster. They make noises, they warp, they pull, they stick, or they slip. They let you know when it's time to pay attention. And when it's time to pay attention, then you *have* to stop traveling and pay attention.

Alignment is making sure you're both headed in the same direction with equal intensity. You can't have four different-sized tires or even four of the same tires inflated to different levels and expect a safe, smooth ride. This doesn't mean you lose your individuality—each tire is separate and distinct from the other three. Just make sure the shocks are in place to absorb the daily bumps we all encounter as we go down the road.

There are lines of communication that have to be maintained—don't let air or the wrong fluid get in those systems or they won't work when you need them.

Keep in mind this is another safety system. If it isn't properly maintained, you risk accident and injury, not only to the vehicle or your marriage, but to all the passengers it might be carrying as well as to others on the road.

When parts get worn, you have to make the time to stop and replace old systems with new ones. New systems keep you current in your relationship. You know you aren't going to be the same person at fifty that you were at fifteen. Upgrading systems frequently along the way helps you arrive at a ripe old age still purring along. You adjust to small changes instead of waiting for the inevitable breakdown.

A certain amount of pressure is healthy. You have to find out what that is and get in the habit of keeping your relationship inflated to that level. Too much or too little brings early wear or a flat. Learn to pay attention. Excessive speed wears things out. Your model has her own definitions of pressure and speed. Learn them and then learn to maintain them.

Remember that list of chemicals and lubricants? Here's where they come in handy. *"To pinpoint a leak, remove all built-up dirt and grime…degreasing agents and/or steam cleaning will achieve this."*[14]

Leaks occur for many different reasons. If you just try to stop the leak without finding its source, you're going to be finding the same leak happening over and over. In order to find the source of the leak, you'll have to remove all the stuff that has built up around the issue. Check her list of cleaning agents, use one, and then talk about her leak.

Note: To many non-vehicle persons, tires and wheels mean the same thing. When you hear those terms being used, make certain you know which one is being discussed. You two have to develop the same vocabulary if communication is going to work.

Note: Tires show the use of excessive speed in turns, braking and acceleration. They're a great indicator of what may be wearing your beauty down. Check them often.

Cooling

Boy, do you want her cooling system working properly. If it isn't, you have to check several different systems. The same may be true with your wife. Her radiator may be full, but the water pump isn't working.

Problems with the cooling system are divided into overheating or overcooling. You've probably already experienced both with your wife. Overcooling simply requires re-setting the thermostat. Overheating means you run down a list of possible causes until you find the correct one. You can't just throw coolant—in the form of flowers, praise, or dates—at the problem and hope she cools off. There is such a thing as too much as well as too little coolant. You might be supplying enough coolant, but it keeps leaking out. The communication system that moves coolant where it needs to be may be sluggish or non-functional.

The problem might be a quick fix or an overhaul, but you won't know until you start asking questions. Ignoring the problem has huge risks, so keep working at it until you have it solved. Anytime she's overheated you need to check fluid levels and replace any that have been lost. If you live a life with strong seasonal changes you need to pay greater attention to coolant than if you live a milder life.

Note: This is a system under constant use, so expect wear to happen. Nobody should feel guilty about the need for new parts. Get life circulating in your relationship again. Replace the water pump or the thermostat and move on.

A final word about dummy lights. Heed them. Women often are more relational than men. They often are more intuitive than men. That means they know something's wrong before you do, but they may not know *what's* wrong. Heed the dummy light. It isn't the job of the LED to diagnose the problem and fix it. The job of the LED is to raise the alarm. Her information will either be a gift to you or a stumbling block. It's your choice.

You're doing well. Hang in there.

SECTION 2
MAINTENANCE

CHAPTER 12

Routine Maintenance
Part A

WHEN ASKED WHAT relationship-maintenance is, guys are apt to reply "flowers, candy, and date nights," hoping they're getting the right answer. It doesn't always work and they don't know why, but they keep doing it because it works part of the time.

In the world of vehicle care, upkeep is so much more than three multi-purpose tools that do all the work. The same is true for the world of the wife. The check list for a vehicle can be long, but it isn't complex. It's so natural that most vehicle owners succeed. There are plenty of steps in wife maintenance. They aren't complex either. Once they're understood, it's easy to be successful.

The first step is to recognize the nature of vehicle upkeep. It's routine, expected, and regular. Regular Maintenance is simply the expected duties that come with having a vehicle in your life. Regular checks are the norm, not the exception. They aren't reserved for special occasions. You perform upkeep every day: check the fuel gauge, check the engine temp, see how dirty the exterior and interior are getting, check mileage to see when the oil needs to be changed, and check the battery.

Note: Requiring maintenance is *not* the same as being high maintenance. Too many guys think doing anything to support the relationship makes the wife high maintenance. Not so.

What exactly is routine care? Whatever it takes to keep the relationship operating well on a daily basis. It comes down the three basic categories: check things, change things, and re-fill things. Flowers and candy are just not mighty enough to do all that work.

Check Things:

Since none of us come with handy dials, beepers and gauges, just how does this work? Think of the time it takes you to check your car. As you walk up to it, you notice if a tire is flat. You get in the vehicle and turn on the key. You check the fuel, maybe note the mileage, check the engine temp, note the need for a wash or vacuum.

Time expended: probably less than 60 seconds.

Tools used: eyes.

Cost: nothing.

Maintenance doesn't have to be long and drawn out.

How do you check things with your wife? You learn her signals and develop communication tools that work for the two of you. (Signals might be no eye contact, head down, or impatience with inanimate objects. This is *not* a complete list. See Steps below to develop your list.)

You have to work at not taking her for granted. Routine care develops communication so you can glance at a few gauges of human behavior and know right away the condition of your wife and relationship.

When you want to know how the oil is doing, you don't just look at the gauge. You "ask" the vehicle by popping the hood and checking the dipstick. When you want to know how the level of friction is between your wife and you, you need to ask her how things are going. We'll build some gauges for you in the Steps section below.

What is termed *routine* changes over the life of your vehicle and should change over the life of your marriage. Vehicles have a break-in period. You drive more slowly, you care for it more often. After a certain period of time has elapsed, routine becomes less frequent. The same principle works here. The first year of marriage requires many adjustments. During that year you develop the communication systems necessary to read your mate. It takes time, but the more time spent paying attention during your break-in period, the better the communication which translates to quick daily checks instead of lengthy conversations.

Change Things:

Think of the simple everyday things you change on the vehicle: oil and filter, tires, batteries, and windshield wipers. You change them because they get worn out. You change them based on actual use rather than a fixed timetable. The goal is to change them when they are used up, but before they are non-functional. Guys want women to be simple to understand and, when you think of them as vehicles, they are. Their needs vary just as the needs of the vehicle do. Run the battery down and it needs to be replaced, even if it was a five-year battery. Run the engine hot for a long period of time and the oil needs to be changed even if you did do it last month.

Even if you just performed some act of care for your wife, if she needs more, then she needs more. Learn not to let her battery run down and you won't have to attend to her needs so often.

A special note about tires: Tires last longer if they're rotated occasionally. If you rotate aspects of your relationship, you don't have to go to the expense of new "tires" as often. Tires are the activities that take you down the roads you travel. Tires change with each decade of marriage. In your twenties you'll travel much faster roads than you will in your sixties. Tires in your twenties might include who does what on the calendar of family activities—grocery shopping, house cleaning, laundry, child care, transport to children's activities, or volunteer work. Remember, *rotation saves wear.*

There are elements in your relationship which are like fluids and keep friction to a minimum. The daily grind of life causes friction. If the daily grind is very stressful, then the fluid *and* its filter have to be changed more frequently. Keep in mind this is *routine*, not extraordinary.

Re-fill Things:

There are vehicle needs that have to be re-filled on a regular basis—air in the tires, fuel in the tank, oil if it runs low, water in the radiator, and wiper fluid.

Note: The nature of these re-fills is not all the same—oil, fuel, air, water, cleanser. Trying to accomplish all fill-ups with one multi-purpose liquid is silly. That's exactly why flowers and candy don't always work. You have to learn to apply the correct remedy to the correct need.

Since re-filling is meant to be routine, it isn't the grand gesture. Nobody gives you a parade because you fill the tank with gas. It's everyday. It's being responsible. Relationship refills are the words you say, the manners you use, and the consideration you give more than any gift of flowers or candy you produce. It's not expecting the house to look like a guy's locker room. Put the toilet seat down, pick up the dirty underwear, leave the bathroom clean. Put the food away. Be considerate.

Whichever Comes First:

Part of routine care is being flexible. The philosophy of vehicle maintenance is that some issues need to be addressed regularly but "regular" can arrive as a function of time or it can happen because of the season or use the vehicle goes through.

The wife isn't any more complicated than the vehicle in the concept of Whichever Comes First. If life is especially stressful, she needs more upkeep. She isn't high maintenance, any more than the vehicle is. When life is routine, support can be postponed for longer periods of time. Enjoy the ride.

To determine her mileage you have to notice how many things are happening in her life that put her under stress. But don't stop there. Not all vehicles are the same. A Cummins diesel is not an MG. They have different load levels. Your expectations of load can't be the same for the MG as they are for the truck. If you bought the vehicle, you bought the specs for that vehicle.

Every vehicle manual has specific steps and tools used for each tune-up or maintenance activity. The required activity may be a blend of do-it-yourself and hiring the work done. You can check your own tire pressure and fill them, or you can have it done. You can even rotate tires yourself, or have it done. But you have to take tires in to have them balanced. The same is true with the needs of your wife. Some of her needs can be met by others. Some have to be met by others. Some you need to do yourself.

The requirement of routine care is not a demand for you to do it all. It's an expectation that you make sure it gets done. When routine upkeep isn't performed, there are always consequences. Running out of gas is more easily fixed than replacing a cracked block, but it still trashes your schedule. Make sure the steps get completed.

STEPS

1. Check Things. When you get in the habit of checking, you always know where you are.

If maintenance is supposed to follow a routine, then establish one. You need to personally prepare for maintenance. You don't try to change the oil when you don't have enough time or are too tired. Don't work on your marriage under such circumstances, either. If you want the best, give it your best. Learn to check every morning and every evening, just as you check your vehicle as you begin and end your day of driving. I'm using driving metaphors here—see Chapter 15 for the translations. Learn to check for:

   a. Overheating, both coolant and lubricant. What's her mood and what's the source of it?

b. Mileage—how long has it been since you rotated tires, changed filters, or re-filled coolant or oil? Write the dates down.

c. What's her fuel level? How burned out is she getting? (See Appendix III Stress Level)

d. Support—does she have enough support (air in her tires) to carry her through every place she has to go today?

e. How's her vision? Check the weather she has to travel through (rough day at work) and make sure her wipers can do the job. Make sure the fluid level is enough so when she gets splashed, she has something to clear her vision and continue down the road safely.

f. List the stresses she's under this week. Write the date down. Keep an eye on how hard she's running because of them. If the stresses go too long and she begins to show signs of wear, schedule a time with her to change things.

2. Change Things. Schedule time to fill her energy. Remember not all maintenance is done by the owner. You're still being responsible if you encourage her to get her nails done or whatever fills her tank. Each model is different. Ask her to list what drains her and what fills her so you know the appropriate remedy for the specific need. Also, know you aren't responsible to take care of everything for her. She's responsible for herself.[1] We all tend to neglect good care of ourselves. Your job is to encourage her to slow down and meet her own needs. You don't have to personally manufacture the fuel; you just have to make sure she gets a fill-up on a regular basis. So that you can know these details about her, have her fill in the following:

Five things that sap my energy (driving conditions, length of trips):

1.

2.

3.

4.

5.

Five ways I act when I'm feeling low (sluggish, poor handling):

1.

2.

3.

4.

5.

Five things that restore my energy (new fuel, new vision, new grip on the road):

1.

2.

3.

4.

5.

Five things that smooth the friction between us (make the oil change last longer):

1.

2.

3.

4.

5.

Five things that cause friction between us (run the system between us too hot):

1.

2.

3.

4.

5.

When you have all this information, you have your own personal gauge and dipstick to check daily so you know the condition of your relationship.

3. Refill Things. Remember some things need to be re-filled often (fuel); other things need it less often (coolant, wiper fluid) Ask:

   A. What five things can I do on a regular basis to fill you back up?

1.

2.

3.

4.

5.

   B. When you come home at the end of the day what one thing could I do to make you know that I'm glad you're home safe?

1.

   C. At the beginning of the day what one thing can I do to give you energy to get through your day?

4. Whichever Comes First. Have an attitude that, no matter what's on the list in what order, *Whichever Comes First* is what needs to happen. Always keep in mind how unique your model is. That's why you're building this list. It fits her and her alone. What fills one personality type will definitely drain another type. The list you've developed here

is just the beginning. Boredom isn't something you want in your relationship. Faithfulness is invaluable. The fine line between the two can only be known by performing routine maintenance. Ask her if there's anything I've left out of this list that's necessary to her on a routine basis. Write it down. Remember this is your custom manual.

5. Give Yourself Permission to Learn.

Remember the first time you changed the oil? It took you longer than it does now. The first time you do marriage maintenance will take longer than it will in the future. The first several tune-ups are skill-building times. Don't expect a one hundred-percent success rate. Remember the VW bus and expect parts to be left over. This won't be your comfort zone at first, but you'll gain confidence every time you perform the steps and use the tools. Remember, however long it takes and however much it costs, it's less than if you don't do it.

Tools:

The tools used in this chapter are largely ones of asking good questions and listening to her responses. In order to get good information, you have to have an attitude that says the process and the information are valuable to you. In order to have the best attitude, use these two tools as an attitude check.

1. Read this definition of love often. Change your attitude to fit this definition. *Don't* change the definition to fit your attitude.

Love is patient.
 Love is kind.
  Love isn't envious, boastful, or proud.
Love isn't rude, or self-seeking, or easily angered.
Love keeps no record of wrongs, doesn't delight in evil.
 Love rejoices with the truth.
  Love always protects, always trusts, always hopes, always perseveres.
  Love never fails.[2]

2. As you think about goals for yourself and your marriage, remember to use this tool: *The <u>only</u> thing that counts is faith expressing itself through love.*[3]

Shortcut:

If all the above is too detailed, how about a few seconds, three times a day? The number of seconds depends on your model, so start with thirty seconds and work up to ninety to see where her working range is. Remember this is routine, so make it both easy and informative, something you can do every day.

1. Morning: Ask what's on her list for the day; express concern that her day goes well. If her love language is touch, then touch while you're talking; if it's words of affirmation, then tell her how her skills will help her during her day; if it's acts of service, then carry something for her to the car or take out the trash, or wipe up the counter, or…you get the idea. Thirty to ninety *seconds*.

2. At the End of the Day: When the two of you meet again at the end of your day, look directly into her eyes and ask how she's doing. Keep eye contact. Option: give her a kiss that lasts thirty seconds and tell her you're glad to see her. Tweak this for her love language, but in all variations, keep the eye contact.

3. Bedtime: Hold her. Thirty to ninety seconds. No words. Kiss her goodnight. Again, be willing to tweak this for your bride.

CHAPTER 13

Routine Maintenance
Part B

THERE ARE TWO parts to the Maintenance Schedule; routine maintenance and tune-ups. Maintenance happens on a calendar basis—daily, weekly, monthly, or a *Whichever Comes First* basis. Tune-ups happen on a mileage, and/or *Actual Wear* basis.

Routine maintenance is different during the break-in period than it is for 40,000 miles. After several years of marriage—when jobs are settled, home is defined, children are birthed, routines and roles are established—new skills are required. What hasn't been resolved begins demanding attention. If it doesn't get satisfied, it may go underground and erupt in divorce years later when you turn fifty. Deferred maintenance buys you trouble, not time.

The skills you came into your marriage with won't be enough to last; just as the skills you had when you first bought your vehicle had to grow beyond the basics of remembering to fill it with gas and check the oil. That was fine then, but along came the need for a little wheel balancing and tire rotating. Then, uh-oh, timing, pistons, rings, and chipped paint. Then came the questions: *Seems like a lot of work. I don't know how to fix it. Is it worth it? Do I hire the job done or do I learn to do it myself?* In order to keep what you have, you have to grow new skills.

Once you make your initial choice, they're all used models and you take on someone else's problems. Work with what you have and you'll be blessed. *Bless—that's your job, to bless. You'll be a blessing and also get a blessing.*[1]

A great marriage takes daily connection, regular dating, and regular getaways. Keep the marriage strong on a daily basis. Unexpected curves, bridges out, detours and some very rough roads lie ahead. Extreme Driving Conditions happen to everyone from time to time.

Once you're on a rough road, it's too late to catch up on the maintenance you should have been doing, so say to her *"I love you, I'm thinking about you."* in some way, on a regular basis, in her language. She can't read your mind and know you're thinking about her. Show her. Tell her.

A word about goals: one of your goals needs to determine the quality of marriage you want. Your effort reflects your goal. If you're both satisfied with a simply being married, wonderful. If you want a great marriage, your maintenance schedule will be different, your definition of *regular* will be different. Neither one is right or wrong.

Why am I harping on this issue of "regular?" You don't grow apart all at once. **Divorce begins when you stop doing the regular maintenance.**

Every day, each of you is changing just a bit while you're apart. If you don't check the mileage, pretty soon you've missed too many routine maintenance times without being aware of it. Big threats are easy to recognize; obvious threats solicit obvious responses. It's the little *daily* bits that blow the engine. The engine is a sealed system—big bits don't get in. There are easy ports for gas, oil, antifreeze, wiring and transmission fluid, etc. All the systems work to maintain the heart—the engine—so you don't have to tear it down. You have to maintain it, though.

Remember, routine is just that—something you accomplish on a *regular* basis, be it daily, weekly, monthly, or annually. Learn to listen to your engine and do the work that is primary, not the easiest. If the engine is knocking, inflating the tires won't help much! You can do this. I know because I'm a mom.

Daily:

Goal: To maintain awareness of present and future needs for attention.

1. Make time to reconnect.

Each day, as the two of you go off in separate directions, you change. If you don't take time to communicate what your day was like and how it affected you, you grow apart. Without the habit of regular maintenance, after a few years of marriage, you stop spending time with each other. You become roommates instead of friends, lovers, husband and wife, one. You stop giving your strength wholly to each other. Outside interests take priority over being together. You dress up for work more often than you dress up for each other. Pillow talk becomes *zonk*.

When you come home each day, take time to reconnect. Not *"How was your day?"* but *"What happened to you today? How did your day affect you/ change you/challenge you? How did you get dinged today? What made you laugh?* If you don't keep up with the small daily changes, you wake up one morning with a stranger next to you. You need to ask *"How can I change with you?"*

How frequently you communicate and what tools you use are up to you, but the maintenance *needs* to be done. Routinely.

Daily maintenance is walking, talking, re-connecting. It's pillow talk before you go to sleep. Time is one thing you can't un-waste. Nobody ever died and regretted spending more time at work. Choose wisely. Look at your daily planner and reserve time for each other. Make it non-negotiable. Decide that nothing eats up your special time together.

2. Pay attention.

The biggest part of daily maintenance is observation, not conversation. Read her gauges—eyes, facial expression, tone of voice, body language, hair, and clothing choice. Don't make this more difficult than it needs to be. We aren't talking the full psychological profile of emotions here. Try *happy/not happy*. (See the page of emotions in Appendix III.)

When you turn the key on and the dash lights up, do you actually gather information from the panel or just put it in gear and go? **Read her panel**. You don't have to talk, just notice. Scan the systems that need attention. The gauges on your dash are there because they represent systems which require monitoring *every time you use the car*. Relationships have a few systems which also require daily awareness. Not lengthy discussion. Not tools and grease under the nails. Observe and integrate acquired information. You add fuel because the gauge is low. Observation is followed by action. You observe many times before you perform any task. Pay attention to her.

3.   Look at her and really see her.

Check for dings and scratches in the paint. They happen to both of you. Somebody says something at work: *ding!* Somebody calls with unwelcome news: *scratch!* Dreams crash, goals fail. If you don't talk about them, you don't share them. If you don't share, you grow apart. By sharing, they become part of your together-story instead of something which eventually drives you apart.

Sometimes you live with dings and sometimes you choose to work them out. That's a separate maintenance issue, not a daily one. Unfortunately, asking, *"How was your day?"* only results in the mass-of-informational response, *"Fine."* You have to go beyond saying the words. The goal isn't to ask the question. The goal is to gather accurate information.

4.   Stay out of ruts.

How do you avoid ruts? Learn to ask good questions. Remember to listen with your Pink Hearing Aid. You may prefer to count grunting as communication, but try to up the bar a little for your bride. You didn't win her hand by being non-communicative. No book can list what works for the two of you. The key for you is always each other. Ask, *"How should I ask you about your day?"* Chevys, Mercedes, and Jags will all answer differently. Then listen. Don't try to fix. *Listen.* Stop doing. Look at her. *Listen.* Write down her answers so you won't forget.

Note: Listening doesn't cost you any words. Just be sure you pay attention.

If she needs you to actually help fix something, she may wail she doesn't know what to do. Every time she says *"I don't know what to do!"* isn't necessarily a request for you to step in. It doesn't mean her mind is totally blank and is just waiting for you to fill it. It may mean she has three choices and can't decide between them. If you just listen, she'll talk herself into one of them. If you try to tell her which is best, she'll likely get angry at you for not listening.

Girls—if you just need his ear, then tell him plainly, *"I just need to talk."* He can relax and listen. He won't get frustrated because you're not taking his help, and you won't get frustrated because he isn't listening. Don't try to change each other. Find a way to communicate.

5.   Know where you're going and why.

One last bit of daily maintenance is your goal. When you go out for a drive, you have a destination in mind or at least a purpose. Just going for a drive is a valid goal. The point is you know where you're going and why. Know the same thing about your relationship with your wife. Goals are determined at a separate maintenance tune-up, but you live them out day to day. Defined goals, reviewed regularly, keep you from traveling too far down wrong roads.

Goals aren't wishes or dreams. They're clearly defined objectives with steps to accomplish them in a defined time frame. For example: *Regular dating for us will be playing a game of cards together every Friday evening.* It takes time to establish good goals. One time I had a refrigerator full of food that needed to be cooked. Hours later, as I set the cooked food on the table, I realized with a shock that I hadn't even tasted it. I didn't know if what I was serving tasted edible! The reason? My goal had been to cook the food so it wouldn't spoil. I succeeded. But what good was all my effort if the food wasn't enjoyable to eat? When things go wrong in your relationship, re-examine your goals and see if you're working just to get something done.

6.   Establish regular dating.

You have to define what *"regular"* and *"dating"* mean for the two of you. It doesn't have to be expensive. Take a ride together, walk around the block, sit in chairs and eat a cookie, or play a game. It can be different every time or a routine you follow. It's up to the two of you. Just do it.

7.   Establish regular conflict resolution.

Allowing anger in your relationship is a gift you give each other. When you permit each other to express anger in healthy ways, you give each other the gift of getting over it, whatever the conflict is about.

When you have a relationship where anger isn't okay, you stuff angry feelings. They don't disappear. They fester, grow, and erupt later. This how-to is covered in depth in Tune-up #4. For now, know that you have to make room for conflict resolution on a regular basis. Make a commitment to each other. Tell each other that you want your marriage to last a lifetime and unresolved conflict won't support that goal.

This is done most easily when you're newly married and don't have a backlog of stuffed Stuff. Remember, you're making life the way you want it to be. Fine tune this agreement and then stick with it. Good intentions have to adjust to Actual Wear.

Your goal for conflict resolution may read something like this: *"Any time we're <u>really</u> upset with each other, we'll tell the other person we need to talk. We'll tell what we're upset about. That doesn't mean we have to solve it right then, but we will get it out on the table for discussion. We have a lifelong marriage and unresolved conflict won't achieve our goal."* Remembering to put conflict in relation to your marriage helps let go of the need to fight to win or to be right. Conflict is a healthy part of marriage if it gets resolved. It's your choice.

I promise this gets easier with practice. Hang in there and keep trying, keep tweaking. I'm proud of you.

CHAPTER 14

Whichever Comes First

MAINTENANCE COMES IN many forms besides Routine. *Based on Actual Mileage, Severe Driving Conditions,* and *Whichever Comes First* are all variations of Routine Maintenance. What's the difference?

Routine activities are calendar based. You do them daily, weekly, monthly, or annually. The calendar alone just doesn't cover every circumstance, so we have *Based on Actual Mileage.* It doesn't matter if you just did the maintenance. Every time the odometer turns over so many clicks, you're supposed to stop and check things over. A week at the beach relaxing isn't going to be as hard on her as a week commuting on ice, with a presentation to give at work, cookies to bake for a party, lunch with the boss, and Fido sick in every room in the house. The week at the beach spent maybe twenty-five miles; the week at work spent maybe 500.

Besides *Routine* and *Based on Actual Mileage,* there's *Severe Driving Conditions.* The calendar may only record one day. The odometer may only record twenty-five miles. But that one day was a blizzard, after dark, on an isolated stretch of road. The wife recorded high stress.

Note: The definition of *"severe"* rests with her, *not* with you. She's the one racking up the miles, out in the weather. I remember the first few times I drove on ice. My knuckles were white, hands glued to the steering wheel, teeth clenched, and if anyone had tried to get me to talk, they would have had their head snapped off. That was *Severe Driving Conditions.* A few years later, it wasn't. Why? Because every winter I drove the same conditions. What began as *"severe"* changed to routine. What she calls severe will change every decade of your marriage because she'll grow more skilled at handling tough situations.

Finally there's *Whichever Comes First*. *Whichever Comes First* is a phrase from vehicle manuals instructing the mechanic to perform a list of checks under one of two conditions: after a certain number of miles or a certain number of days, whichever comes first. The intent is that the maintenance in question needs to be checked often. You can't claim that because you just checked the oil last week, you shouldn't have to check it this week even though you drove across the country and back. If the miles were used up, then it's time for a check-up without any complaints. You can't say it isn't time. You can't expect the need for maintenance to be put off. Don't get so stuck on being right that you cling to a list instead of life. You're expected to modify and customize your list of activities based on how fast you burn up the road.

Note: She's the keeper of the mileage. You get to keep the calendar. *She* has to tell you how hard the miles are for a particular day, week, or month.

Note: Remember—it's *her* load and her strength. She isn't wrong because she doesn't carry her load the same way you do.

During the first year of vehicle ownership, maintenance is required often. This is the beginning of *Whichever Comes First* maintenance. You can't go as fast as you're capable of going. It seems like every time you turn around you have to baby the engine through its break-in period. You do it because you know if you take it easy in the beginning, the engine will give you years of strength.

After the break-in period is over, actions that needed frequent attention in the beginning become necessary less often. If you do the *Whichever Comes First* stuff as it becomes necessary, you don't have to schedule major repairs as often. It's like the dentist telling you you're doing such a great job brushing and flossing that he doesn't want to see you for awhile. Barring *Adverse Driving Conditions*, what you've learned to do routinely keeps you humming down the road with only minor stops.

I hear whining out there. Don't get caught up with self-defeating talk about how long all this is going to take or how much it's going to cost. However long it takes and however much it costs, it's less than if you don't do it. Even serious-sounding items on a check list still only take a moment to check. Check the oil? How long does a glance at the gauge take? Popping the hood and pulling out the dip stick? Sixty seconds max. Oil changes? Thirty minutes. Make the time to do it. We all have twenty-four hours. It isn't magic or luck. The ones who succeed at marriage make the time for success. Keep a mental picture of the shock on the face of the guy whose bride walked out. There's a reason he's shocked and she's gone: routine maintenance. It's your choice.

Remember, we're talking about checking here, not a full-blown engine re-build. It's the same with balancing your checkbook or doing your taxes—leave it to once a year and it's a mess. Do it regularly and it takes less time and stress. It isn't the job's fault; it's your attitude.

Unfortunately, doing your best includes baggage. You can be very sincere and still be wrong. We'll deal with baggage in Tune-up #3. For now, realize we have choices about our baggage: rebel, acknowledge or ignore it. We probably do a bit of all three.

Remember that definition of love? Let's look at it from a different interpretation.

Love never gives up.
Love cares more for others than for self.
Love doesn't want what it doesn't have.
Love doesn't strut,
Doesn't have a swelled head,
Doesn't force itself on others,
Isn't always 'me first.'
Doesn't fly off the handle, doesn't keep score of the sins of others,
Doesn't revel when others grovel,
Takes pleasure in the flowering of truth,
Puts up with anything,
Trusts God always,
Always looks for the best,

Never looks back,
But keeps going to the end.
Love never dies.[1]

We all fail at love and we all have choices to make when we fail. Rebellion and denial cost both you and those you love. Choose to have an attitude of solving and re-solving issues instead of ignoring them. Make resolution a goal. Hold each other lovingly accountable. Work hard at resolving issues so you don't have to watch your family suffer the consequences of your choices. As one pastor said to the bride and groom, *"As you walked down that aisle, you made the last independent choice of your life."*

You can't have both independence and *inter*-dependence. The benefits are supposed to outweigh the sacrifices. Sometimes it's hard to remember. Discuss the consequences of poor choices with each other. Share how your choices affect each other. Knowing makes you stronger if it helps you make better choices.

Note: If you choose to do nothing, **you're still choosing**. We all inherit weaknesses from our parents. We can choose to use our inherited traits as an excuse or change our overall inheritance into a legacy. Strength doesn't come easy. The generations before you sacrificed to pass on the good they knew. Do the same. *Whichever Comes First* means you deal with it.

Note: In all this rah-rah, cheering-you-on stuff, please also accept Grace. If any generation could attain perfection and pass it on to the next, we'd have world peace. In the real word, we simply need to do the best we can with what we have, when the opportunity comes and still love each other. Remember, *"The only thing that counts is faith expressing itself in love."*[2]

CAUTION: Saying the words, *"I don't ever want to do that again."* doesn't necessarily mean I won't ever do that again. It may only mean I don't want to get caught or pay the consequences, not that I've decided to change my behavior. Your communication with each other needs to address the blindness we all have towards ourselves. Develop the skill and self-discipline to lovingly call each other on your inherent dishonesty and rebellion. *"I care too much <u>not</u> to say something to you about this..."*

Why? Because we don't really repent of some of our sins. For example, we stop having sex before marriage because we get married, *not* because we confronted the attitudes and small daily choices that led us to such a choice. We want something better for our children, but they observe our attitudes and come to the same conclusion we did at their age. We wonder why they act that way when we *"taught"* them sex outside marriage is wrong. We taught the rule apart from the personal discipline necessary to achieve it. We modeled small daily choices of rebellion while expecting obedience from them. The seed we sow yields true fruit.

We desperately need honesty from each other to have any hope of knowing why we end up where we do. True love means telling the truth *and* walking the consequences together. It's a gift to have someone in your life who's going to be there when you need to grow.

Note: CAUTION: WARNING! I said *lovingly*. We'll disappoint, anger, betray, and deny the very ones we love. If venting anger were healthy, every wife-beater would be a portrait of serenity. Stuffing anger isn't the solution either. *"Go ahead and be angry. You do well to be angry—but don't use your anger as fuel for revenge. And don't stay angry. Don't go to bed angry."*[3] I didn't say it was easy. Revenge is sin. Rudeness is sin. Chilling silence is sin.

One problem with being angry is that we often do to the other person exactly what they did to us! If it's so wrong, then why did *we* just do it? To be able to be angry *and* not to sin is the freedom of being legitimately angry about something and then getting over it. No more passive-aggressive anger. No more stuffing anger. No more blowing up and then being stuck with the same problem. Being honest with each other is a huge gift. Give it and receive it.

Honesty is healthy. *"I'm so hurt by what you said/did"* is a true, honest statement. *"You're a jerk, louse, etc, and I never want to see you again. Don't touch me or talk to me ever again"* may also be honest and still not be true.

You have a relationship worth fighting for. Just remember the opposition to your marriage comes from within more often than from outside. Everyone guards against the obvious big things that hurt a marriage. It's the little things that quietly erode and kill the relationship. You have to know and overcome your own temptations and weaknesses. You have to overcome your own anger and desire for revenge. You have to want to restore the relationship more than you want to retaliate, be right, or vent your anger.

Having said all that, overcome your weaknesses. Solve your problems. Be as open about your weaknesses as you are about your strengths.

STEPS

1. Check her mileage—how hard has she worked this week, doing what?

2. Check your attitude—prepare yourself to take responsibility to maintain, to learn, to handle baggage.

3. Check her load capacity—is she an MG or a diesel or somewhere in between? Adjust your expectations accordingly.

4. Maintain honesty—start with yourself. Be honest about who you are.

5. Work on improving your expression of anger. Make it a goal—define what you want to change; list the steps you'll take; make a schedule; insert some accountability; celebrate.

CHAPTER 15

Daily Maintenance
Or, Losing the Remote in
Your Relationship

A GREAT MARRIAGE takes daily connection, regular dating, and getaways. Keep the marriage strong daily. We've discussed *Routine* and *Whichever Comes First* aspects of wife maintenance. Now let's look at what's supposed to happen daily.

We maintain vehicles every day and don't give it a second thought. Every day? Yep. Before you step out the door you've handled three routine checks: keys, wallet, and a goal.

As you approach the car, you check three more conditions: tires—flat? Exterior—scratches or dings? Environment—obstacles in the driveway? That's six checks before you open the vehicle door. It wasn't drudgery.

You get in and begin a new check list. Turning the key in the ignition, you check gas, oil, and mileage: three checks. Fastening your seatbelt, you check the need for wipers and lights. Two more checks, that's five. Then you survey the interior for two more checks. The clutter check reveals how much longer you can put off cleaning duties. The other check sets your comfort: turn on the tunes, set the volume, and adjust the temp. It's all automatic; no real thinking about it. Because all systems are tuned and working, your daily upkeep requires little effort. With one glance, you know how far away the next oil change, fuel stop, and tune-up are. You make a mental note, turn the key, listen to the engine for a second, and check that you have what you need to achieve your goal: checks six and seven. Off you go. Lots of maintenance steps in a few seconds.

Maintenance of a wife is the same, something you need to do each day until it becomes automatic, a quick scan of a few vital bits of information. Regular checks change your attitude toward the rest of the routine schedule. Daily upkeep gives you confidence so you don't put off the 250 mile/weekly checklists. Because you know her so well on a daily basis, the bigger duties aren't so off-putting. Let's translate the daily automatic stuff.

Do you have your keys? You hold the key to her heart because she married you. That means you have responsibility for where she goes with you and the condition she arrives in. Even though you hold the key, you still have to take the initiative to put it in the ignition and start the car. You have to take the initiative to open the door and sit in the driver's seat. You have to take responsibility in order to enjoy the ride. Don't misplace that key. Locks can freeze up and she can refuse to let you in if you neglect her too long. You probably have more than one key to operate your vehicle. You have more than one key to your wife's heart. One of them is romance—whatever you did and said during courtship. You already know that works. Keep doing it. Keep improving it.

Do you have your wallet? You carry more than money in your wallet. You carry a license, an insurance card, and somewhere you carry a registration. That license and those cards mean commitment to her and to a set of rules. The rules are there to keep the two of you safe and to keep the world you live in secure. If you want the rights of ownership, then you have to take responsibility and that means paying the bills. In marriage, the rights of marriage come with responsibilities and debts. You can't have a healthy one without the other.

Where are you going? You have a goal in mind every time you get in the vehicle. You need to know your marriage goals just as clearly. Dragging her along to fulfill only your goals won't work forever. Be united in your goals. Goals imply a destination and a plan to get there. Direct paths? Rough roads? Do you brave hazardous driving conditions together or do you protect her from them? There isn't a right answer. Every choice has consequences. Maturing growth happens under the most severe conditions.

So do break-downs. Talk it over together and plan according to your mutual strengths and weaknesses.

Check your tires. Remember it only takes one flat tire to keep you from going somewhere. If she's a little flat, don't suggest she wait to replace what is worn until all four tires are shot. You benefit most from being proactive. Regular checking, rotating, and replacing prevent ninety-nine percent of flats. What causes tire damage? Being out of balance, high speeds, excessive braking, and driving over hazards instead of going around them. Check frequently to see how the road is treating her. Remember it's *her* rubber meeting the road, not yours. You can't tell her how it ought to feel.

Exterior: Check her out—is she dressing the way she dresses when she's happy? Remember what make and model you're dealing with. Chevys don't dress the same as Jags, but they can both look spiffy. How's her hair, her smile, her eyes? If the luster isn't there, then start asking diagnostic questions to find out why. The earlier you ask, the easier the fix. Usually.

Obstacles: Is there anything in her way? When the two of you take off, is there anything obvious in the way—a bike, garbage, a curb, a child? Take time to deal with any obstacles to your goal. Obstacles are easily removed by parking the relationship in a designated place every time. When you park the car in the garage and close the door each night, obstacles don't usually accumulate to stand in your way the next morning. Taking preventive care in your relationship eliminates so many problems.

Are there Warning Lights? Again, it's your responsibility to check fluid levels. She's telling you, but *you* have to read the gauge. The old dialogue of, *"You never told me!"* followed by *"Yes I did!"* comes to mind. We won't go into why they're called dummy lights. You have to read, interpret the information, and plan accordingly. You have to make sure the engine temp is okay and the battery is charged. Check the fuel level. Her information is available. You have to take the time to read it.

Seatbelt fastened? You need a certain amount of self-imposed restraint to drive safely. You need a band of safety that leaves your hands and head free to move, but keeps your heart in a safe place. That means you have to be aware of your imperfections and be honest about them. Love is patient and kind. It isn't jealous and rude and doesn't seek to have its own way. It isn't selfish, proud, or boastful.[1] If you don't buckle up but do crash, both of you get hurt. Buckle up with a code of conduct that helps you be the best you can be. It's far too easy to be the least you can be.

Wipers/lights: It doesn't take much to adjust to the exterior environment— just a button or knob—but it's vital to your safe travel. Don't label the need to adjust as a threat to your esteem and make stupid choices. Adjust. Remember there are _two_ sides of the glass to maintain. Just because you scraped the ice off the outside doesn't mean you can skip running the defroster on the inside. If things are chilly, do both.

Interior clutter/cleanliness: The interior tends to get cluttered. Clean-ups are easier if they happen more frequently. Spills become stains and lingering odors if left too long. Loose dirt becomes a stain if it isn't cleaned off. Pay attention. Be proactive instead of waiting until you're forced to do something.

Note: Sometimes the things you do away from the vehicle or relationship linger. A smoker might never smoke in the vehicle, but because clothing, hair, and breath all carry the smell, when they get in the vehicle, it smells like smoke. If your activities bring home unhealthy aromas, change what you're doing.

Note: Hanging an air freshener tree from the rear view mirror is _not_ a substitute for cleaning. No, it's not. This is your mother speaking.

Note: If you're going to use vehicle rides for discussion, make sure the vehicle is clean enough for her to ride in. An exhaust leak might be perfume to you and toxic to her. A seat full of dog hair on the passenger side is fine when the passenger is a dog. Clean it up for your wife. You cleaned up for dates, continue the courtesy and clean up when taking her for a ride.

Comfy? Atmosphere is important. You set the tone with the tune you sing and the volume you use. Make certain that levels and styles are adjusted for your _mutual_ enjoyment and comfort. In order to do that, you have to know her preferences. Take time to learn them, write them down. Learn what you do or don't do that sets a tone in your relationship. Most of us are clueless about how our behavior affects those around us.

Maintenance steps

Remember that daily maintenance is just checking. Before you head out the door each day check the following:

1. Keys: Does she light up when her day begins? Even if your days begin separately, you can leave her a note to let her know you're thinking of her.

2. Wallet: Remember your responsibility to love, honor, and cherish with your finances and loyalty to a code.

3. Goals: Remember where you're going—a great marriage—and don't take detours.

4. Tires: Does anything look or feel flat? If so, schedule a time to pump things back up.

5. Exterior: How's she looking? Compliments do wonders. If you notice scratches or dents, schedule time to polish the relationship.

6. Environment: Know what obstacles are in her way—that means looking at her calendar, at life from her perspective.

7. Gas, oil, mileage, warning lights: How long has it been since she had a boost of energy? Is there friction in the relationship causing heat? Remember, you're just checking. If the warning lights are glowing, schedule time to support her.

8. Wipers, headlights: Can you see where you're going? Remember there are two points of view on the windshield. You can scrape the ice all you want and still not be able to see if the interior is fogged up. Check to make sure your vision is clear. Make sure *both* of you see clearly.

9. Interior clutter: Because this is a relationship, you have to check your interior clutter *and* hers. Everyone has weaknesses. Know

yours and know when it's time to deal with issues. Ask for feedback on this one.

10. Tunes, temperature, and tone: The atmosphere of the day is something you choose. You're not a victim. You choose songs of complaint or of praise. You permit things to get chilly or hot. Too much bass or treble can be jarring. Together they're harmonious. Check your atmosphere and adjust it daily for everyone's comfort.

Tools:

"Husbands, go all out in your love for your wives. Don't take advantage of them"[2] Practice going all out in your daily checks on your relationship. Practice daily checking for a month until it becomes as second nature as all the checks you do when you get into your car. Your vehicle routine is your reminder. When you grab the vehicle keys, think about your keys to relationship. When you adjust the temp or the music, think about the atmosphere between you and your wife. The more you use the tool, the more skilled you become.

CHAPTER 16

Weekly, Every 250 Miles
Or, Fueling

GOAL: HAVE FUN together.

Date, date, date. Tell her it's a date. Treat it like a date—something you invite her to join, something where she has the option of saying "No." It isn't a right, it's a privilege. Take turns choosing the date so she doesn't resent always doing just what you want and never what she wants. Then for pity's sake, *be* a good date. Remember, you're doing it to be together. She doesn't always like what you want to do, either, but she does it.

Sometimes it's a dress-up date. (That means you dress up, too.) Some models like to dress up more than others. You look so handsome when you're all decked out. It melts her heart. She *needs* to have her heart melted once in awhile. By you. Don't make her wait for a funeral or wedding to see you looking all suave and debonair. (Don't make her go to books or movies to get her fix, either.). You like it when she's all dolled up, right? But it's lonely for only one to get really dressed up. It takes two.

Notice her looks like you did during courtship. If she's a manicure sort of model, then give her a gift certificate to have her nails done. The fact that you noticed, and *did* something makes her shine twice over. You can bump up the points by telling her to get her nails done because you're taking her out on a date. You've extended her good feelings from the moment you presented the manicure all the way through the date and the memory afterwards. That's a lot of happy connections all over her wiring.

Note: You have to know *your* wife. Not all models want manicures, salon hair-do's, spa times, etc., but there's an equivalent for your model. Ask.

CAUTION: Make sure she understands *why* she's getting this gift. Your gift can be mistaken to mean you think she's a mess. How do you avoid the trap? Tell her how to interpret your gift. Say something like *"I wanted to do something special for you and thought you might enjoy _____. Go have fun, Beautiful."* This will earn you romance points all day long and you don't even have to be there!

Note: Hair, nails, and new clothing trips are often group activities. Expect her to need to have a friend along. You don't pay for the group, or be the one to go along, but you do need to leave her time to grab a friend to enjoy your gift.

Back to dating: remember the goal. If the goal is to date, then it won't matter what happens on the date. You went on a date, therefore you did your duty and all should be fine. Right? Wrong!

The goal is *not* to go out weekly. If that's the goal, then it has nothing to do with the relationship. It's like knowing that the car needs gas, taking it to the gas station, and then not filling her up—a waste of time because the goal was defined wrong.

The goal is to maintain your relationship. The date is just one way of achieving that goal. The movie can be lousy and you can still enjoy being with each other. So, tell each other what your best date was and why. Also discuss your worst date and why. Now you have the tools to have successful dates with each other.

Guys often see courtship, dating, and romance as the tasks done prior to marriage. Once the goal of marriage is accomplished, they see romance as no longer necessary. That's why you have to make a new goal of determining what kind of a marriage you want and what you'll commit to doing to attain that marriage. Thinking you're done with romance or that it only needs to happen on Valentine's Day or your anniversary is wrong. Different models have different expectations here, but to leave out romance entirely is wrong. Unless you don't want sex.

She wants romance as a prelude to sex. He wants sex. He gets it. She doesn't. She loses interest in sex. He loses interest in her. She starts reading romance novels and watching chick flicks. He starts looking at other women. They talk to friends instead of to each other. They dress up for co-workers instead of for each other. They make time for meals with co-workers, but are too busy to eat with each other. Two people who could talk all night before marriage now talk less than fifteen minutes out of 1,440 minutes each day.[1] They become roommates. Conversation is about schedules. The guy is attracted to someone at work and—get this—*talks* to her at length. The woman talks to her girlfriends. Two lonely people live together until they don't. They wonder how they got so far apart. It begins by not taking time to talk and date.

Remember what I said earlier. *"Date"* can mean anything. *"Date"* means you get out of the house. *"Date"* can be a walk around the block. It can be a ride together. *"Date"* can be a picnic, a movie, or sky-diving. Take classes. Go places. Eat out. Plan it. Let it be impromptu. Do whatever the two of you enjoy and can afford. Plan a picnic in front of the fire on the living room rug.

Note: Dates you can't afford aren't dates; they're weights that drag you down.

Lack of dating kills communication. Don't let this happen to you:

"Honey, can we talk?"
"Whadda ya wanna talk about?"
"I don't know. I just want to talk!"
"Well, then talk!"
Sigh. *"How'd your week go?"*
"Ok."
"What did you do?"
"Hey, I made widgets. The game is almost on. Are you done?"

When you hear this conversation, heed it as a warning light. Your engine is about to blow. Check for loss of intimacy. Stop being so busy immediately and change the way you're doing life together.

There are some good sources of conversation starters out there. As we move into this text-messaging age and put one more screen between us and others, our conversation skills are going out the door. If you need suggestions, Google "conversation starters" for suggestions, but try to keep your relationship so vital that you don't need the helps. You didn't need helps during courtship, did you?

During courtship, you just *had* to talk to each other as often as possible every day. I'm not suggesting that rate should be your normal setting. Just don't let the skill and passion dwindle until you have nothing to say to each other and need helps.

Steps:

1. Choose a place and time for your date.

2. Invite her. Prepare in any necessary way (tickets, babysitter, ordering the picnic, making reservations, filling the car with gas.) Some of the most memorable dates Hubby took me on were simple picnics after work. Two bagels, a tub of salmon cream cheese, some fruit, and wine were the menu. Nothing complex. Oh—and the candles. Don't underestimate candles. He put the candle in the cup holder (cracked the window open), poured the wine, put the placemat over the console and—Ta-Dah! Instant picnic in the truck with rain pouring down. We'd drive to someplace with a view and relax together.

3. Talk. Enjoy each other's company. It works. Try it or some variation of it. Use your head to make it work for the two of you. Oh—don't forget the music, either. Let the tunes set the atmosphere. You're doing great.

CHAPTER 17

Monthly, or Every 1000 Miles Or, Detailing

Goal: De-clutter the relationship.

CARS, LIKE RELATIONSHIPS, tend to accumulate clutter. Relationships, like cars, have different levels of clean up. Accumulated stuff tends to be small things we ignore, which build up to a full-blown squeal or stain if left un-tended.

Sometimes you have to look under the seat to find stuff which has conveniently rolled out of your sight. Bend over, drag it out, and evaluate it. Toss it? Move it? Whatever your choice, change its place in your relationship before it comes rolling out during an *Extreme Driving Condition* and causes a wreck.

All of us accumulate stuff to a different degree, so the depth of your cleaning depends on how much clutter you've accumulated and what your level of clutter-tolerance is. You'll also find you tend to accumulate the same sort of clutter over and over. That doesn't mean you have to give up eating chips in the car. It means you should get very good at cleaning up crumbs before they leave the little grease stains on the seats and elsewhere.

Sometimes de-cluttering reveals the need for a major tune-up. Don't ignore the needs, and don't try to do both at the same time. Simply note that the tune-up needs to happen and schedule it for later. Keep on task with de-cluttering.

How often you take care of the grime is up to you and your bride. It's far healthier to set aside time to discuss issues rather than grow increasingly frustrated. Passive/Aggressive models—those who are kind, tolerant, and sweet right until they aren't—are especially prone to letting important issues slide. Trying to be nice, or gracious, or good is admirable up to the point we say, "*It's okay*" when it isn't. The presence of resentment and anger are warning lights your clean-up isn't happening often enough. We're being dishonest with ourselves and with our mate. To diminish the number of blow-ups, develop the habit of talking regularly. Talking before anger and resentment set in also develops trust so you *can* talk about issues.

Don't let your relationship get to the point that if someone asked your bride to write down every unresolved conflict in your marriage, a book would result. De-cluttering regularly keeps the list short and not so depressing.

If clutter builds up, then the clutter itself becomes a trait of your relationship. You become part of a demolition derby, in one crisis after another, instead of having a destination.

Choose the habit of de-cluttering instead of dealing with issues only when a crisis forces you. Your marriage story will be either all the stuff you haven't solved or it will have the reputation of being problem-solvers. Once you form the habit of resolving issues, the issues themselves lose importance because your confidence in each other and in yourselves increases.

Tasks:

1. Determine the type of clutter. Make a list. Some clutter requires a vacuum. Some requires upholstery cleaner. You won't necessarily use the same tool each time, but the goal of de-cluttering needs to be accomplished.

2. Choose the appropriate method of clean-up. It might be talking/listening, it might be doing jobs around the house, or making an

agreement about chores or schedules—the method depends on the type of clutter.

3. Mutually dedicate the time and place for de-cluttering. Then do it. Ask questions. What are some of our un-resolved issues? Can we solve them or do we need to accept our differences? Are they a problem? Do you see them becoming a problem in the future? Do we just need to talk this out? Do we need a book? A counselor?

Note: *Do not* de-clutter on a date. Keep at de-cluttering until the job is either complete or a later time of maintenance is agreed upon. Note all needs for tune-ups and schedule a separate time and place.

4. Finally, celebrate your accomplishment. Celebration is sort of like waxing. It makes the work of de-cluttering last longer. It protects against some of the pitting and fading that naturally happens. And it's purely optional. Just doing work makes one type of memory. Celebration after a task makes a different memory. You choose your own memories here. You'll look forward to the job or dread it based on how you choose to go about it. If you celebrate, you'll add that memory to her wiring. Trust me and do it.

Note: The difference between maintenance and a tune-up is mostly in time. Washing the car doesn't take much time. Buffing out all the little chips and repainting is a major operation. If your de-cluttering turns into a lengthy process, then you're probably working on a tune-up. Reschedule your time and reassess the need.

CHAPTER 18

Annually or Every 13,000 Miles Or, Programming Your GPS

Goal: Systems Check.

WHEN GUYS ARE asked to rate their marriage on a scale of 1 to 10, the scores usually come in around 7 to 8. When their wives are asked the same question, the scores come in much lower, often around 3 to 5.

Because women are connected with wiring to the entire vehicle, they tend to be much more aware of breakdowns before men are. They're the dummy light of relationships. Listen and heed their awareness. You need to ask out loud how you're doing. Remember you're both on the same team. This isn't adversarial any more than the oil light coming on is a giant condemnation of your car ownership. Pop the hood, check the oil, fix the problem, and get going again.

You need to ask in a non-manipulative way:

Right: *I honestly want to know how you think we're doing.*

Wrong: *Hey, on a scale of 1 to 10 we've got about a seven, right?*

Allow me to stereotype for a moment. Women tend to want to please. Men mistake pleasing for honesty. Women can get trapped into being good or nice, right until the moment they blow. Men tend to like the system, but not the results. You'll save yourself many a mid-life crisis, and an empty nest meltdown if you'll make honesty part of your relationship.

For instance, there's a huge difference between wanting me to be with you and you wanting to be with me. Guys are happy when their bride goes where they want to go and does what they want to do. Aren't we all? But there's another side to the story. You also have to enjoy being with her and doing what *she* likes to do. It has to be a two-way street.

Look over your past week/trip/expenses, etc. and see how many decisions— how many actual miles of life lived reflect *your* decisions, values, and goals, and how much was spent on *hers*. Ask for her input—it's like checking the oil instead of relying on the glaring red light shining in your face.

People think truth hurts. What hurts isn't the truth; it's giving up the lie. Truth comforts after it hurts. The issues you won't face don't go away. They fester and come back with a vengeance. A new mate isn't the answer because you carry with you half of what was wrong with the first marriage into the next one. Dealing with everyone's stuff isn't easy, but it's healthy. Let go of the illusions.

We tend to use mirrors to evaluate self. Mirrors are wonderful, but not always accurate. Sit down together with your checkbook and look at where your money is flowing. Does what you actually spend reflect your goals and values? If not, there's likely conflict between you and your mate. Look for the inconsistency, and resolve it.

Children are another great mirror, especially when they're small and don't know better than to imitate you, literally. It doesn't do any good to yell at them for misbehavior if you're a daily living example of what you don't want them doing. Chanting *"Do as I say, not as I do"* doesn't work. Mates, speaking in love, are the best reflection of who we are. However, we can often have pieces of self we don't share, don't want known. There's a way to deal with that part of ourselves, too. I like the Psalm which says, *"How can I know all the sins lurking in my heart? Cleanse me from these hidden faults."*[1] Spend time with God. Be open to what He reveals.

One more analogy—when you look at your gas gauge, you want accurate information. You don't want soothing words or vague estimates. You need to develop gauges that give you accurate information so you can make wise decisions. Tell her when you need this type of information from her. Then be ready to adjust your plans based on reality rather than perception. If the gas gauge says it's empty, you don't pretend it's full and keep driving.

Most of maintenance is simply checking. You've achieved your goal if you've checked. However, checking is meant to reveal problems before they become break-downs. Checking is not a substitute for performing actual tasks. Checking reveals things that are worn out and need attention. It works like this: you scan the fuel level and read one quarter of a tank. You mentally note the need to schedule time to stop and refill. Checking alone doesn't fill the tank.

Sometimes a monthly task happens at the same time as a tune-up. Twelve thousand miles happens at the same time as the every-six-month check up. Whether or not to double them up is up to you two—just remember that the goal is *not* to do the work. The goal is to build a great marriage. Keep in mind what you want your marriage to look like.

I know this sounds like I'm saying the same thing over and over. I am. In the auto manual, you're instructed to check the same thing over and over.

Systems which function every day have to be checked often. You can't check the oil once and then expect to never check it again. The systems of a marriage must also be checked again and again at regular intervals. Get in the habit.

Steps:

1. Review personal, marriage and parenting goals; values; recurring conflicts; and personality issues. Take a getaway for just the two of you. If money is a problem, stay home, turn off the phone and TV, and send the kids to grandma's house for the weekend. If you go to the shop to check systems, you have to clear away distractions. You don't go to the shop to change the brakes, then turn on the Super Bowl,

and have all your children's friends come play in the shop at the same time. Dedicate your time.

2. Look at your checkbook. Fill in the time chart in Appendix III. Where do you actually spend your time and money?

3. Look at the behavior of the children. What are they mirroring to you? Don't yell at *them*—change *your* behavior. They followed you into bad behavior; they'll follow you into good behavior.

4. Refer to the manual where you've recorded personal and marriage goals, values, parenting goals, personality type, and VIN. Check to see if they still fit the two of you. Discuss any changes. Record them.

5. Celebrate.

SECTION 3
TUNE-UPS

CHAPTER 19

Tune-up #1
Or, Humming Down the Road

TUNE: "HARMONIZE, *AGREE*, *adjust*, sing, melody, rhythmical succession, *agreeing in pitch*, an air, a tone, *to change one's tune*, to sing a different tune, a standard of pitch, *to adapt to a mood or condition*, to tune in—*to adjust to receive*, to tune out—*adjust to eliminate interference*, to tune *up—adjust to same pitch*, to *adjust to proper or required condition (motor)*, hum"[1] (italics, mine)

Mileage: First year of marriage or later, whichever comes first.

Goal: Learn who each of you is.

Let's start with a definition: *"adjusting to the proper or required condition"*. What do we mean by "adjusting?"

Maintenance is mostly checking, something you could cover during a date or a truck ride. It's providing materials necessary to do a job. Tune-ups are more involved. They require focused attention until a standard is achieved.

Minor tune-ups are maintenance plus replacing worn parts, like belts. Major tune-ups involve everything in a minor tune-up plus replacing worn parts like valves.

Maintenance fits with the flow of your day. Tune-ups take focus and concentration. Major tune-ups take time. **Both types are necessary.** You can't do them over dinner or sitting at the movies. They take dedicated time—maybe a weekend, maybe a week.

Tune-ups are the time to make changes in your relationship. When do you do them? It's nice to be proactive and schedule these things, but life doesn't always allow such planning. After any life transition—a move, new job, births, deaths, new home—plan for a tune-up. *Actual Wear* produces the need for a tune-up. If you're experiencing a lot of overheating, then you need to change something before you crack the engine. You can be proactive and schedule the time or you can wait until things break down. Remember: breakdowns are both more costly and time-consuming than scheduled activities.

With vehicles, tune-ups are scheduled on the basis of either time or distance. In your marriage, schedule your tune-ups the same way. When you go through a difficult season, schedule more maintenance and check carefully for the need for a tune-up. When life becomes routine again, focus on maintenance.

The word "tune" brings to mind music. A tune-up produces harmony. It requires adjustment, tuning *in* to receive, tuning *out* interference. It requires the two of you working together. It means taking the time to listen. It means working until you find agreement. Some marriage issues are minor tune-ups—easy to discuss and find your hum. Other issues are more involved and require much more work, the same as with the vehicle.

Doing this work when it's scheduled instead of waiting until it's needed is so much better. You discuss instead of argue. You talk as friends, working on the relationship instead of as adversaries on either side of a problem.

WARNING: Don't try to make changes while you're driving any more than you'd try to change the oil while going down the road. Remember, there are appropriate places to do this kind of work. Go there. Too many women do the relationship work and too many men let them. Don't go there.

The process for all tune-ups is simple: check, remove, install, and test.

Always check before you start making changes. *If it ain't broke, don't fix it* is a good guide, up to a point. If it's worn, make changes before the break happens. Signs of wear? Same as the car—squeaks, rattles, sluggishness. Crankiness, silence, tears, tiredness.

After installing a new system, test it. Just because the guy at the parts counter said your new approach works, that doesn't mean it succeeds for you and your bride. Install it, check it again, make any adjustments, and test it again. Keep at it until you hear the hum you want in your relationship.

Tune-up #1 defines personal values, marriage values, personality type, love language, and… Goals, both individual and marriage. It's important to do both. You aren't your marriage and vise versa, but your marriage is part of you, so pay attention to it. Your marriage goals don't have to be profound, but they will guide your choices. If you don't make goals, your choices are made for you by those around you. Live *your* life, don't let others live it for you. And don't let this list put you in a box—this is just your way of communicating with each other who you are and how you want to be treated.

If the goal of this tune-up is to understand each other, then you have to have a way to take your new knowledge with you so you don't forget what you just learned. Write it down. Date it. The information will change, which is why you keep coming back to it. Work with what you have until it changes.

Next, with any goal there have to be steps taken or your goal won't go anywhere.

One step is a commitment to supporting the individual goals and values of your mate and the common goals and values of your marriage. How will you do that? Saying, *"I commit to supporting you"* isn't enough.

This is where you both have to define what support will look like. Ask. Listen. You're doing this tune-up after a year of marriage for a reason—you have a year of experience. Tell each other your stories of support success like this: *"I felt so supported by you when I had that bad day at work and came home and you said/did… I felt like I could go back and handle the situation because I knew you were in my corner." Or, "I knew our marriage was important to you when you said…"*

One of the best support stories I have for Hubby was when Grandma was sick. I'd flown to California to take care of her. I was going to be there a long time. My days were spent trying to find documents, meeting with doctors and nurses and actively advocating for her care. After a week, I was worn out. Hubby drove down to help. When I got back to the house he was out running errands. I went to the bedroom and on the floor he'd placed his big shoes on either side of mine. No note, no words, didn't involve flowers or candy. It meant so much then and he still gets points for doing it.

Because we often go about life in our own bubble, you also have to, gently, discuss the times you didn't feel supported and why. *"I felt alone when this was going wrong and you said/didn't say…"* But don't just leave it there. Don't expect to have your mind read. Teach. *"What I needed to hear you say or have you do was _____."*

There needs to be a commitment to values for your marriage *and* a specific plan for how you're going to maintain those values. You'll re-evaluate what you've written against the realities of life on maintenance breaks during the coming year, so don't obsess about getting this "right." You'll repeat and fine-tune this activity many times during the course of your marriage. The point here is to get something down so you can begin to use it.

Steps:

1. Set aside a time and place to share and discuss the following information.

2. Fill in the Values Grid (Appendix III). Trade results and discuss. Why did you choose one value over another? What does each value mean to you?

	Her Values	My Values
1.		
2.		
3.		
4.		
5.		

3. Fill out the Values Grid (Appendix III) for your marriage and discuss.

	Her Values	My Values
1.		
2.		
3.		
4.		
5.		

4. If you have children, fill out a Values Grid (Appendix III) for your family and discuss. Have each family member circle their top five values, then tally them. You'll find five common values that you all share. Post them on the fridge. Frame them with your family pictures. Talk about them as a family.

	Her Values	My Values	Our Values
1.			
2.			
3.			
4.			

5.

5. Fill out the Personality Type test (Appendix III) and record type and the corresponding explanation of that type. Discuss.

Her Type:

My Type:

6. Take the Love Language test (Chapter 8), record the results and discuss with each other.

    Her Language   My Language

1.

2.

3.

4.

5.

7. Gauges: Have her fill in this chart with her specific likes and dislikes. Fill it in because you'll forget.

GAS	OIL	TEMPERATURE	BATTERY
quick fill-ups	add a quart	add water or anti-freeze	add water
Cards	Go for a walk together	Ask: How was your day?	You look great!
Flowers	Clean the kitchen		I'm sorry.
candy	Do Laundry		
	Take care of dinner		

8. Write a goal for your marriage and for yourself that you want to accomplish before your next tune-up. Include the time frame and the steps necessary to reach the goal. See Goal Sheet in Appendix III.

Our goal:

    Steps:

        1.

        2.

        3.

Her goal:

    Steps:

        1.

        2.

3.

My goal:

Steps:

1.

2.

3.

9. Define regular dating. Write your definition down.

10. Write up a conflict resolution agreement. See a Sample in Appendix III. Write it down and date it.

11. Celebrate your accomplishment.

Note: This tune-up involves a lot of paper. If you want, fill in the grids, charts, and tests before you two get together so your away time is spent sharing rather than filling in charts, grids, and tests. This information is meant to be a baseline for future tune-ups. Record all the information gleaned in this manual. Then use it.

Whether it's maintenance or a tune-up, neither of you can do this work alone, just as you can't do a tune-up without the vehicle. Tune-ups are involved. If it gets to be too much at once, modify it to suit your schedule. You may have done some of this during courtship. Hooray! You still need to gather that information into one place so you can work with it in these tune-ups.

This was a big first step. Good job.

CHAPTER 20

Tune-up #2
The Drive System:
Strengths and Weaknesses

MILEAGE: AFTER YOUR first year of marriage or whenever you want to.

Goal: Begin using the information you acquired in the first tune-up.

Evaluate your past year together. Now that you know what your strengths are, it's time to look at your weaknesses.

Many times our strengths are our weaknesses. We're so strong in one area we tend to see things from one perspective, and that makes us blind to other ways of thinking. Our strength means we prefer to operate in that area. Which means we don't *want* to do things in a way that isn't as comfortable—in other words, someone else's way.

You're no longer single and you aren't the dictator of a country. You must learn to use your strengths for someone else's benefit. I don't want to be harsh, but it's called growing up. We all need to do it and it's hard for everyone. It's also optional. We can actually make it all the way to death and never grow up. But...not growing up means we've dumped responsibility on others all our lives and haven't reaped the rewards of maturity. We can't have it both ways. You have to be mature enough to look at your immaturity.

Knowing your weaknesses actually makes you stronger. Instead of bulling your way through life, you're able to steer clear of a few more disasters because you know that when you do X or Y, negative Z often results. By having discussions with your mate, you learn that if you do X—your strength—at a different time or in a different way, you get the result you want, with the bonus of approval and cooperation from others instead of the Z's of resentment and resistance. It's like installing a performance chip on the engine—you're still pressing on the same gas pedal, but you're getting more power because you're using the power in a different way.

Know your weaknesses. The attitudes you take for granted—meaning you've never examined why they're there—come out lots during the first year together. Wedded bliss suddenly bumps up against two different styles of living:

But my dad <u>always</u> set the table while my mom fixed dinner!

My mom always folded the socks like this!

You're supposed to clean up after yourself in the bathroom!

And, of course, there's the toothpaste squeezing issue. *And* how you spend holidays, vacations, and get-togethers with family. Whether we always clean house together as a family first thing Saturday morning or sit and watch cartoons while watching cold cereal on the living room floor. Who pays the bills and when and how often. And on and on. And on.

Your personality types and values are the keys to resolving this stuff without daggers and power. If you look at the DISC sheet you finished in Chapter 3 you'll see values listed for each personality type. (See Appendix III) Compare them to the values you chose from the values chart. They match. Amazing isn't it? (If they don't match, then consider re-taking the personality test or recognize that none of us fits in convenient little categories.) Your basic motivation is different from hers, so what you value is going to be different.

Note: I said *different*, not better.

Talk about where your strengths are a great help to each other. Discuss where your strengths have overpowered each other. Discuss where you've relied on your mate's strength instead of growing your own. If the discussion gets tense, know that you have some conflict resolution to do. Ask permission to deal with it at another time if necessary. Don't let it distract you from the goal here—to learn how to use this information to achieve your marriage goal. Then set a time. Don't slough it off by saying, *"We'll talk about that later."* "Later" almost never comes. Honor each other by keeping the promise and resolving the issue.

WARNING: One of the most common tendencies when encountering each other's weaknesses is to try to "help" the other person change. It won't work. We all have areas we need to change. Bad habits and family dysfunction detract from marriage. What we're discussing here is basic personality. Stay focused with me here. Marriage is not permission to change each other.

I don't want you to feel boxed in here. Personality flexes as you age. When you first leave home, who you are often reflects who you have been *taught* to be in your parent's environment. As you establish your own home, marriage, and work life, there will be new pressures to conform to. Some you'll embrace and some you'll reject. What you choose will change your goals and values and, in some ways, your personality.

Every decade of life will bring new choices and new conformities. You finally learn how to be a success in your twenties and, tada, you turn thirty with an entirely new set of challenges. It happens every decade. Get used to it. You need to monitor values, goals, and personality on a regular basis, just like you monitor the gauges on the dash. After the first year, review them with the goal of making sure they still fit. Review them after every period of *Extreme Driving* or *Actual Wear*.

You've seen how personality drives your values. Let's take this one step further. Your values drive your goals. There can be a lot of emotional attachment here and a lot of baggage.

One of you comes home from work full of enthusiasm.

"Guess what?! I had this bright idea! So I bought/sold/did/said/called/ invited…"

Can you hear the wail? *"You did what?!"*

One person values action, the other values planning. The bright idea became a goal and goals require action. Right? Wrong. Sometimes they require action. Other times they require collaboration. Tune-ups are the time when you learn to tell the difference and equalize to achieve your "hum."

Goals are based on our values. Sometimes we aren't aware of them. This is where you two are a huge asset to each other because you help bring goals into the open. Recognized goals are less likely to cause conflict because nobody is surprised by them, and your mate can *help* you reach your goal. This is a partnership, remember? Un-communicated goals cause conflict because your mate, being unaware of your expectations, isn't supporting them. The lack of support may look like obstruction and BAM, you have conflict. Avoidable, *unnecessary* conflict. You'll have enough of the unavoidable kind anyway, so take time to protect your marriage by getting your goals defined.

Do you see why you have to _know_ this information like you know your social security number? This isn't head knowledge; this is a working tool to make your marriage better *if* you'll use it. Help each other remember. Commit to knowing this about each other. Post it on the fridge and in your wallet. Make it part of your PIN or password. Write it down. It'll come easier with review.

CAUTION: Hold this information lightly. The details are not the dimensions of a box. Everyone needs room to breathe, to grow, and to be inconsistent. We're biological, not mechanical. If a vehicle can be full of surprises, leave room for people to do the same. That's why you review the information on a regular basis. If you don't take time to review it, you'll have more conflict because your assumptions about each other will gradually become wrong.

"But you always _liked_ waffles for Saturday breakfast!"

"Well, not anymore."

Honest feedback is called for here. We all have illusions about ourselves.

Have a goal sheet for each of your top five values. Why? Because you subconsciously have expectations about your values. If I'm getting cranky in the afternoon, I do a values check. Which value hasn't had attention during my day? I may have spent all day valuing order (cleaning house) and not expressing health (getting outside). My crankiness says it's time to switch effort over to my unmet value. Please **Note:** *I* am responsible for my mood. I'm not waiting for someone else to "make" me happy. And that leads to the next point about making goals.

An important part of setting goals is looking where affirmation comes from.

If my goal for, say, losing weight, is dependent solely on the scale, I'm doomed to failure. If the measurement of my success is only the scale, I'll be disappointed several times and be tempted to give up. If my method of measuring success is broader, then my success will be greater.

Losing weight in and of itself can be a dead-end goal if we do it for a person, for a party, for approval. Let me say that again. We lose weight for approval. So make sure the source of approval is in your corner, not external to you. Don't let three numbers on a scale determine your self-worth. The people at work, the party, the reunion may not notice that single pound you fought so hard for and then your goal is fried. If, however, I'm losing weight to develop a new healthy normal, then the scales are only part of my affirmation. The week of self-discipline which didn't result in a pound lost is still a success. If I walked every day and walking was one of my tasks, I succeeded. I don't need someone else to tell me I succeeded. The goal was a new healthy normal and a week's worth of health is definitely success, irrespective of the scale. Week after week of a healthy lifestyle eventually impacts the scale, encouraging me to stay faithful to my goal. Though dieting is more a female construct, you need to understand all the wiring that goes into it so you can understand and support her.

Accurate goals take time to figure out. For now, just start writing down what you know. Come back to it later and see how your goals can be defined better, or steps clarified. See if your goals took you where you really wanted to go. Also be willing to dump the goal all together. Sometimes we get confused between who we think we are, who we want to be, and who we actually are. If the goals just don't happen, then maybe you really aren't interested.

Don't set goals based on guilt. Be honest with yourself. The choices you make throughout the day support *your* goals. If they don't, either you need to quit trying to please other people, or you need to change your goals.

Steps:

1. This is a tune-up, remember? That means it takes time, so step one is to schedule a time and place for uninterrupted talk.

2. Review the goal. Know why you're doing this: to gain understanding about each other.

3. Quickly review the information from Tune-up #1. Is it still accurate? If not, communicate changes and write them down in the manual. Date them.

4. You're doing this tune-up after a year of marriage so you can relate the information to *Actual Miles* of your relationship. Share how you see your strengths becoming weakness. It's important to tell your mate you know you mess up. Don't make her tell you. And it's important for her to tell you where she knows she messes up. Ask for help from each other. *"When you see/hear me doing this, would you give me a little signal to help me stop?"* This is the honesty that builds a strong marriage. Guard it. Commit to it. Value it highly. And for heaven's sake, be a cheerleader for each other, not a judge.

Give honest feedback. To practice this skill in the beginning, confess something not too vital. If we practice on small areas, we gain skills necessary to change more entrenched weaknesses. In marriage we turn a blind eye to some things. But, when a problem is recurring, you or your mate may have to confront before it does damage. Think of this as stroke, poke, stroke. Affirm, compliment. Phrase criticism as encouragement. There's more on this in conflict resolution. Again, don't get distracted from your goal for this tune-up. Practice using information.

5. Write down goals for each of your values. Share how you can support each other in achieving those goals. Be specific, give timelines and steps. The more you communicate, the more cooperation you get, the more success you enjoy.

6. Repeat this process after *Extreme Driving Conditions*, *Actual Wear* or annually, whichever comes first.

7. And celebrate. Don't forget to celebrate.

CHAPTER 21

Tune-up #3
Your GPS: Where Are We Going?

Mileage: First year of marriage or now, whichever comes first, or about three months after Tune-up #1. Don't get hung up on this timeline. If in the first three months of marriage you've graduated from college, moved to a new city, and started a new job, don't let a tune-up add more pressure. Just don't blow it off, either.

Goal: Begin defining what kind of marriage you want and the steps necessary to achieve that goal.

What do you want? Is the goal to make the marriage last? That could mean you just survive each other. Not fun! A good marriage? A long-lasting marriage? A healthy marriage? How about having a mutually satisfying marriage? There isn't a right answer, but the steps will be different, so take the time to really *think* about what kind of marriage you want.

Plan. It used to be said, if you don't choose your morals, your friends will. This is true of goals as well. Going to and from a job each day is not a goal. To *have* a job isn't a sufficient goal. It has no direction. It's just marking time. Know *why* you're going to work, each day, both personally and as a couple. Make sure the job supports your marriage goals, and values for both of you, otherwise you'll get to retirement feeling like you wasted your life.

Having a happy marriage is do-able, but it takes some well-defined goals and well thought-out steps. A goal without specific steps to achievement is just a dream. It won't happen. Also, a well defined goal keeps you steady during *Extreme Driving Conditions*. Goals and tasks have to be reviewed often to make sure they still fit the two growing, maturing individuals they support and to remind you of what you're working toward.

A good marriage won't just happen. A good marriage can come to an end if it isn't maintained regularly. You're capable of success. Go for it.

Note: In forming goals, if you only focus on what you *want*, you'll be disappointed. If you focus on what you can *give*, you'll find greater contentment.

Marriage is about giving, not taking. Let me say that one again. Marriage is about giving, *not* taking. *Your marriage vows were what you promised to give, not what you expected to take.*

When marriage partners focus on their rights and their expectations of the other person, the marriage is in trouble. Unfortunately, too often, daily life degenerates into taking. Good morning, I have a need. Leave the bedroom and bathroom a mess for her to pick up, and where are my clean shirts? What's for breakfast? What's for dinner? Where's the remote? Pick up after me because I worked all day.

This scenario translates to the marriage being all about you. It won't produce a strong marriage. It's supported by her vows to love, honor, and cherish and yours to just provide. There's one thing wrong with the provider role—you work to earn a living even if you weren't married. She would never wash *your* socks if she weren't married to you.

Give. Give of yourself. Give your time, energy, and strengths to take care of *her* needs. Pick up after yourself. When you act like a rebellious teenager leaving a mess in every room for someone else to pick up, your roles become unequal. Your actions weaken your marriage. Ask her where the marriage feels unequal. Ask her where she feels you give and where she feels you take. Listen to her. Give her feedback. Discuss. Make changes. Practice doing this over and over.

Give to your marriage and it'll give back to you in abundance. Take from your marriage and it'll run dry.

Take a marriage check-up online. It's like hooking up the diagnostic computer. It gives you information. Information doesn't condemn you; it gives you power to make changes.

Guys don't want the diagnostic because they don't think they can fix whatever is wrong. That's the same reason a woman drives to a safe place with steam pouring out from under the hood—she doesn't think she can fix it, so she drives until she can get help. Both scenarios risk destroying the engine. The solution is just a matter of tools and education. Go for it.

Steps:

1. Set aside time together to define what you want your marriage to look like. Do something you both enjoy. Let conversation be part of your activity. Dream. Romance. Encourage. Be honest. And remember, styles change. What you dream in your twenties won't be the same in your forties.

   a. Over the coming decades, what you value and need from your relationship will change. Build in flexibility and ambiguity. Build in not having everything the way you want it and living with that. There's a big difference between accepting and tolerating. Add commitment to your list—to dating, to conflict resolution, to having fun, to personal growth, to being honest, to having fun, to growing old together, to having fun, to loving each other, to having fun.

   b. Did I mention having fun? Do you really *want* to live with someone the rest of your life and *not* have fun? Then commit to it. Make it happen. It won't happen unless you plan for it.

   c. Decide what outside influences you will and won't allow. Decide what books you'll read and discuss together. Decide who you'll go to and who you *won't* go to for advice. Decide where the in-laws fit into your picture.

   d. Decide who plans dates, how often you go on them, and how much they cost.

e. Decide how often you will or won't go on couples' retreats.

f. Decide how you'll decide! Remember that the *two* of you are *one* couple. When you disagree and one person loses, the marriage loses. Always. Half of the relationship can't lose and have the relationship win. More on that in Tune-up #4.

g. Decide who will do what and how often you'll re-negotiate that list.

This is not an all-inclusive list. You have to make your own as you go along. Start with the goal sheet. Date it. Write it down. Commit to reviewing it annually. Commit to reviewing the steps you write down monthly. Go for it!

DATE:_____

GOAL:_____

We want to have a _____ marriage.

We'll measure our achievement by (See Appendix III):

1.

2.

3.

4.

5.

In order to achieve our goal of a _____ marriage, we will:

Step	By date:	Done by
1.		
2.		
3.		

4.

5.

We'll review these steps monthly and adjust as necessary. We'll encourage and support each other by listening, being honest, loving, and…

We'll have fun together!

CHAPTER 22

Tune-up #4
The Electrical System:
Conflict Resolution
Or, "It is useless to put on your
brakes when you are upside down."
Paul Newman

MILEAGE: FIRST YEAR of marriage, now, three months after Tune-Up #3, or whichever comes first.

Goal: Committing to rules of conflict to guard your marriage.

Resolving conflict involves vocabulary—words like *Fine, Nothing,* and *Okay.* It involves what our friend Doug calls his Pink Hearing Aid. It includes all that stuff you've been working on: personality, family history, values, goals, components, and wiring. It might even include tears. Mostly it involves listening. And that's why it doesn't come easily to most of us.

I'd love to wave a magic wand over this area of human relationships, make it easy, and guarantee success. But you know what? Without struggle, we don't become strong, like the chick emerging from the egg. It takes work to grow up, to become more kind, mature, and loving. We all need to do it and the only way is by learning to successfully resolve conflict. There's no way around conflict. I haven't always believed that.

The main goal of this tune-up is to develop your particular guidelines for what you want conflict to look like in your marriage. At the end of this chapter you'll make your first of many drafts of a conflict agreement. Throughout the life of your marriage you'll continue to refine that agreement because you'll hopefully grow into a different person than you are today.

The point in this tune-up is that conflict resolution is vital to the health and life of your marriage. When someone tells me they never fight, red flags go up. Avoiding conflict isn't healthy. Avoiding conflict is not even the goal. Why? Because differences are going to happen and if they aren't resolved, somebody has to stuff it. When we stuff our values, opinions, or feelings, they don't decompose. They fester and grow. The real you wants out. After being stuffed, the real you often comes out as destructive anger.

As my friend said, you can't be good friends until you've had a fight. It took me years to understand that, and even longer to trust it enough to put it into practice. That's why I married Hubby. We had a fight. He was honest with me. At that point, I knew this was a good relationship, because we both could be angry and have something good come out of it. The relationship grew *better*.

Conflict resolution is about tools, skills, experience, and wisdom. Your tool kit needs to include knowledge about personality, family history, goals, and values. (See Tune-Ups #7 and #8 for more detail.) Your skills need to include listening, knowledge, and love. Once you understand the basics, they do you absolutely no good unless you put them into practice and keep using them until you develop the wisdom, *not* the judgment, to know how to handle each type of brokenness in your relationship. Your experiences need to be both positive *and* negative so you can learn from mistakes and develop wisdom. Make room for failure. Yes, this takes courage.

Skill #1: Wisdom vs. judgment. Why do I make such a big fuss over the difference between judgment and wisdom? Because one has heart and the other is simply knowledge. Marriage is all about heart. It's living to give rather than to take. Everything you say and do, everything you *don't* say and do is about heart. Wisdom considers human beings and the ripples of any decision. All of your choices, both good *and* bad, impact more than the two of you.

Wisdom combines justice and mercy. Wisdom sacrifices for each other. Wisdom irrationally loves. I don't mean irrational in a dysfunctional way, but in the way one person is devoted to another, regardless, in spite of, *because* of. Wisdom comes from living out that altar promise to love, honor, and cherish until death parts you. Oftentimes human beings unfold into beauty at the most illogical sequence of events, and you *have* to believe that more than you want to have your own way. If there's one thing you want to become in your marriage, it's *wise*. I'd much rather have a wise mate than a knowledgeable one. Wisdom is a skill that comes from applying knowledge.

Skill #2: Knowledge vs. understanding. In conflict resolution two issues come to mind—tears and *"they remember everything."* So, why do women cry? Why do they bring up everything you've ever done during conflict? Knowledge means sometimes you simply accept what you know without demanding understanding. You know how to replace a carburetor without understanding the physics involved, so don't get fussy about using the same principle here.

You already *know* women cry and remember more than you do. Their character traits aren't going to change. One key to conflict resolution is not to try to change the other person. Encourage each other to be your best. That's not the same as encouraging them to be what suits *you* the best. One is manipulative and controlling; the other is a cheering section, a celebration as you strive to achieve maturing goals.

As to *why* women act the way they do, well, that's another book I'm not writing. Remembering the compartments and wiring analogy helps. When you're having a fight over, say, the checkbook, for you the fight is only about the checkbook. You're in one compartment and want to stay in the checkbook compartment. News-flash: she doesn't have compartments. She has wiring. The issue of the check book is wiring-linked to what you did for her birthday, the nail polish she didn't buy, the kitchen tool she bought and didn't like, and on and on.

Obviously, her list will be different from this one, but she doesn't grab one wire and isolate it from the rest of the mass. You do, and not by virtue, but simply because you're built for compartments. You *do* remember all those incidents she brings up during conflict, but they're in individual, separate, compartments. You don't *want* to go to all those compartments. It's too much work. All you wanted to do was to discuss the checkbook.

If you accept the difference between compartments and wiring, you'll be able to resolve more conflict. Her wires are no more wrong than your compartments. You probably won't understand, but that doesn't stop you from acquiring knowledge you can apply.

Part of your conflict resolution may have to include identifying all the wires attached to the checkbook issue. For her, acknowledging that those are part of the issue will often be all that's needed. This is the Pink Hearing Aid—being able to translate wires into boxes and vise versa. Once she has all the wires identified, *then* she can go with you to the issue you want to resolve.

Please **Note**: all the above is a general rule of thumb, not a set-in-stone dictate of women in conflict. Sometimes the issue you want to resolve is just as straightforward to her as it is to you. You don't have problems with those issues. The above statements are meant to help when you *are* having difficulty. Remember, waffles and noodles are both made from the same basic ingredient, flour. You're more alike than different. You just process differently.

Tool #1: The Pink Hearing Aid is absolutely necessary to understand female vocabulary. If you interpret all female conversation literally, you'll find yourself in big trouble. Words like, *Fine, Okay*, and *Go ahead* actually mean the opposite, especially if she's quietly humming, *"God Will Take Care of You."* Please discuss the list of definitions in Maintenance Chapter 10 with your wife so you understand your model's use of these dangerous words. Have her edit the list and add any personal favorites.

As to the tears, well...There are a lot more answers to that question because there are so many models out there. Tears are no excuse for you to avoid conflict. Sorry, but they do tend to come with most models. Her tenderness has two sides and you can't have the part you like—tenderness—without accepting the part that makes you uncomfortable—tears. Tears are *not*, however, permission for her to get her way, or to avoid personal responsibility. How to know the difference? Refer to Skill #1.

Guys feel they have to do something about tears to make them go away. Their definition of doing something involves large movements and slaying dragons.

A lesson learned from boxing—the closer you are the less they can hurt you. Tears often require no words. If you just hold her and let her cry, she'll love you for it. You're letting her cry in a safe place—your arms. Letting her cry in your arms *is* doing something about it. Unless you're the reason she's crying. See Troubleshooting.

Whenever I think of this aspect of women I think of Bernie. During one of our family dramas there was too much for me to handle. I called for help. He came over, took in the situation and held me while I cried. He didn't tell me things were going to be all right. He didn't say *anything*. He just let me cry. What a priceless gift—one I'll always treasure.

Skill #3: Anger. It's a real achievement to be able to be angry: at the right person, at the right time, to the right degree, and with the right attitude. It's wrong to deny anger and it's just as wrong to selfishly vent it, especially on the wrong person. Check yourself on the following list of denied anger. How many do you see in yourself? How many does she see in herself?

sarcasm
silence
lateness
gossip
put-down humor
"forgetting"
fake smiles
sulking
gaming
making excessive noise
not paying attention
blaming

embarrassing people

not respecting boundaries

"accidently" damaging things belonging to others

expecting others to "just know" what you want

having a sense of entitlement

seeing yourself as a victim

using "should," "could," and "would" in your conversation

This is by no means a complete list. Feel free to tell each other your own favorite ways of passive anger.

Denied anger means the people around you have to learn to read you. Instead of looking where they're going, they have to watch you. You're making them responsible for you. That's wearing on your marriage engine.

Skill # 4: Honesty. Women can get trapped into being nice girls at the expense of being honest. But it isn't a one-sided trap. Guys get trapped into being tough instead of honest. It hits both halves of the marriage engine block and you're *both* going to have to help each other overcome it. When you sense she's being nice instead of honest, you're going to have to ask her what she really means. In the same way, when she sees you being all macho, she needs to ask what you really mean.

Honesty actually strengthens relationship. When you're known, you are trusted and respected. By speaking up, you tell others that you care about the relationship so much that you're willing to risk rejection. You give others a chance to explain things from their point of view. You're saying you trust the other person to care enough that one differing opinion isn't going to blow it. In the previous chapter you defined what kind of marriage you wanted. Whatever kind you chose, you can't attain it without honesty.

Tool #2: The Accident Reporting Guide. I really like the five step State Farm accident report guide:

1. "DO NOT notify the police."

Don't notify your enforcers—friends, family, co-workers, etc., when the two of you disagree. First you deal with each other. There's a time and place for reporting to others, but it isn't now. First try to resolve the problem with just the two of you. Involving others just spreads the problem. Turning to others is a red flag. Pay attention to it. If she tells others, find out why. *If a fellow believer hurts you, go and tell him—work it out between the two of you. If he listens, you've made a friend. If he won't listen, take one or two others along so that the presence of witnesses will keep things honest, and try again.*[1]

2. "DO exchange information without trying to determine guilt."

This means use "I" statements instead of "you" statements. *"I felt really bummed when you came home and _____."* instead of, *"You are such a jerk. How dare you come home and _____."*

3. "Sketch the wreck from your point of view."

Sometimes drawing a picture helps. It isn't against the rules to use paper. Remember, your personalities, values, and goals are different. Tell what the disagreement is about from each point of view. Be honest. Share your feelings. There are always two sides.

4. "DO report to your Agent promptly."

If God is part of your marriage, then for heaven's sake, talk with Him about the incident. Let Him be a part of the crisis *and* the solution.

5. Keep a list of emergency numbers:

Human anger does not produce the righteousness that God desires.[2]

If you are angry, be sure that it is not out of wounded pride or bad temper.[3]

Don't hit back; discover beauty in everyone.[4]

If you've got it in you, get along with everybody.[4]

Don't insist on getting even; that's not for you to do. "I'll do the judging," says God. "I'll take care of it."[4]

If you forgive those who sin against you, your heavenly Father will forgive you.[5]

Husbands, love your wives, and never treat them harshly.[6]

Husbands ought to love their wives as they love their own bodies. For a man who loves his wife actually shows love for himself.[7]

Don't let the sun go down on your anger.[8]

Don't rush to confront. Instead, sleep on it.[9]

Above all, love each other deeply, because love covers over a multitude of sins.[10]

Love is patient, kind, gentle. Love doesn't keep a record of wrongs. Love rejoices in the truth. Love is not rude, self-seeking, or easily angered. Love always trusts, protects, hopes, and perseveres. Love doesn't envy, isn't proud, and doesn't boast.[11]

The only thing that counts is faith expressing itself in love.[12]

List your own "numbers" here:

Skill #5: Goals. Remember, the goal is to resolve conflict, not to win an argument. Remember the definition of "tune"—to adjust. Resolution might be neither quick nor easy, but to have the kind of marriage you two want, you'll have to work at it until the job is done.

If your goal is to heal the relationship, then keep at the apology words (Tune-Up #7) until you get it right. The more you practice, the easier it becomes.

Goals are so easy to get wrong, or at least be short-sighted. If the goal is to say the words, then the result, and the relationship, really doesn't matter. What matters is being right—saying the prescribed words to get what you want, which is to win. The insincerity comes through loud and clear. *"There. I've said the right words. Now you have to accept them."* Don't go there.

CAUTION: A discussion becomes an argument when somebody has to win.

You can't resolve conflict without humility. As long as you're so certain you're perfectly right, you won't be able to resolve conflict. Telling yourself you did everything right is a road to loneliness. Nobody does *everything* right. Nobody is perfect.[13]

After you've written your goals, review them every week for the first month or until you begin to memorize them. You need to know the rules for your marriage, just like you need to know the rules you memorized to pass the driver's test.

If you don't practice the skills, you lose them. Why is it we think we can avoid practice and yet do well!? It doesn't work in sports, music, or math. It doesn't work in relationships either.

Tool #3: Rules. You'll probably have a few rules in common: no yelling, no profanity, no abuse, yes to listening, yes to being heard, yes to being honest. Whatever they are, write them down, date them, and re-visit them often. You did this in Chapter 9. Make any necessary changes.

Note: I'm assuming the offended party also wants to heal the relationship. Sometimes you may say the right words, but the wounded one doesn't want to restore relationship with you. It can happen. Don't be naive and assume you can always be forgiven for acting in immature, angry, or otherwise destructive ways. Nobody puts up with it forever. The *"Do it now and ask forgiveness later."* attitude is pretty arrogant and won't work for long. Forgiving is another tool, covered in Tune-Up #7.

Make allowances in your agreement for blowing it. If you plan ahead for how you'll restore relationship, then you already have a plan when it happens. It *will* happen. If you don't make a plan, then you have two crises to solve—the unresolved conflict *and* how to restore a broken relationship. You don't use a spare tire often, but because you plan for a blow-out, you aren't stranded when the tire blows. Your planning and preparation help get you going again.

Tool #4: Storyboarding. When you're stuck, one great tool I've found for keeping an issue as the issue is storyboarding. Write down your expectations, dreams, or whatever, on paper (3x5 cards, sticky notes, or whatever), and put them up on a wall, whiteboard, bulletin board, table, or whatever.

If the two of you are discussing a vacation, then the card at the top of the board is the purpose of the vacation. Is it to relax, to visit people, to see certain destinations? If the goal is to relax, then someone wanting to visit a different destination each day isn't going to be happy. Once that's defined and the dates fixed, then start sticking up the expectations of each person. After you've defined what your vacation looks like, then decide who does what to make it happen.

Lastly, remember to stroke, poke, stroke. Heck, go all the way and just say nice things without the poke!

WARNING: If the only time you complement is when you take a poke, your compliments become invalid. You *can* find something you appreciate about her every day. Tell her! Too often guys tell other guys what they value in their wife and the wife quietly withers from lack of praise. If you hear yourself talking about your wife to another guy, either good *or* bad, for pity's sake stop and take it home. *She's* the one who needs to hear it, not another guy! Communicate how much you value your relationship with her, that who she is and what you have together is important to you.

CAUTION: Keep perspective. Any disagreement isn't about the entire marriage; it's only about laundry, or garbage, or who forgot to write it down. It isn't about her value or worth. The point of the discussion is to safeguard the relationship, not to destroy it.

In all of these tune-ups, remember after the work is complete to take the vehicle out for a test drive. See if any further adjustments need to be made. Make changes. Test drive your changes for a month or two, then come back and review them.

Steps:

1. Set aside time and place for relaxed conversation.

2. Quickly review your personality types and values.

3. Review your goal for your marriage and refine it if necessary.

4. Write down your rules for conflict, date them, and make a follow-up date to review them. (See sample in Chapter 7.) Include in your statement why you chose these rules—to build the kind of marriage you want. Make sure to include steps for restoring the relationship when you've blown it. Ask each other, *"If I were King of the World, how would conflict be resolved?"* Then write down your answers.

5. Tell each other how to make up after a tiff. Tell each other what to avoid. Guys often don't get it that touching a hot wife can send off sparks and shocks.

6. Tell each other what makes you feel safe and what makes you feel afraid during conflict. Tell each other what you need to hear and see. Tell where you feel safest during conflict.

7. Too many men think that going to a public place—like out to dinner—is a great place to tell your mate something is seriously wrong in the relationship. If you're going to confront her, make sure it's in the safest place _she_ knows. *Ask* her where that is. Write it down. Memorize it. Tell her how *you* want to be confronted. Not giving each other this information means you have to learn it by trial and error. That's the stuff that pits the engine. You're actively guarding the marriage when you give each other this knowledge.

8. Say, *"I'm sorry. I was wrong."* five times to each other, just for practice.

9. Goals are great, but unless we review them regularly, we tend to forget them. How many times have you made a New Year's Resolution only to forget it a few weeks later? You've put in a lot of work on this tune-up, so don't waste it. Read what you've written every week until you remember it. Then re-read it once every three months, then every six months. As your goals become an integral part of daily life, you'll need to read them less. Once you remember them you only have to review them annually to update them

10. Affirm, affirm, affirm.

11. Have fun. Celebrate the strength you've just built into your marriage.

CHAPTER 23

Tune-up # 5
Test Drives: Application
Or, "You can get straight A's in marketing and still flunk ordinary life." P. L. Newman to Lee Iacocca after his Pinto caught fire.

MILEAGE: SECOND YEAR of marriage, or now.

Goal: To learn more about each other and marriage (*not* to read a book).

Once a year or so, after you've done all of the *Actual Wear* groundwork of the preceding tune-ups, read a book together. This isn't necessarily an annual thing, but it *is* a scheduled thing. Read a book you both agree on. Take turns choosing the book. Read about the stages of marriage so you can plan for them. It's the closest thing to a GPS system available to you. Read about sex. Read about love. Read about men/women, faith, parenting. Read together. Discuss. Exchange ideas. Grow together. Read with discernment. Have fun. Relax. Remember why you're doing this—so you can have the kind of marriage *you* want. Go for lots of truck talks.

In your choice of books you need to present your side of things as well. Read something like *Wild at Heart* or *The Man Whisperer* so you can explain to her what it's like for you to be a guy. She needs your help understanding you, just as you need her help understanding her. Neither of you is the Average Person. Average is a statistical tool, not a model to follow. Strive to be the "best you," not the "best average somebody else."

What that means is, read with discernment. Every author writes from a limited point of view. Nobody has all the answers for you—not even your mom. God gave you a brain. Use it. Modify everything you read to fit the two of you. Don't modify yourselves to fit a book.

Read these books any way that works for you. Hubby and I often read the entire book separately. He skims. That's his personality. I study, highlight, write. That's my personality. He doesn't have to be like me and I don't have to be like him. Then we look for a good time to discuss, usually a ride together. It might be a local trip for groceries, a trip to Portland for supplies, a vacation, or just a drive. It may take a combination of all that to get through a book. We just don't do as well in the living room in chairs. You have to find your own natural groove. Just be sure it's something you enjoy so you learn to associate this time with good memories instead of drudgery.

Think of the book as a tool. Reading is equivalent to buying the tool. You must *use* what you read in order to benefit, just as buying the wrench doesn't change the oil filter. Don't expect to put into practice everything the book offers. Just because you bought a metric set of tools doesn't mean everything metric in the engine is now tuned. You tune up one system at a time. I'd rather see you develop a few strong skills than not do any of them.

Most books stimulate your interest in only one or two concrete ways. That's why you re-read these books. You have to live life before some of this stuff makes sense. Any book is about a lifetime of that particular topic. Choose one change to make. Tell each other and encourage each other.

Note: I didn't say "hold accountable" because encouraging each other usually accomplishes the same thing, but in a parenthesis of love. Treat her the way you want to be treated: gently, lovingly, with compassion, and understanding. Changes will happen.

Steps:

1. Set aside time.

2. Review as needed: personality, goals, values.

3. Review your marriage goal.

4. Select a book, read, and discuss (see list in Appendix II).

5. Celebrate your marriage. Enjoy each other. Have fun. Be best friends.

Hubby: *This really is like a manual because you can read a car manual but you'll never remember it all. When the time comes for a specific repair or tune-up, you have to re-read the manual! No shame in it. Nobody's expected to remember it all.*

CHAPTER 24

Tune-up #6
Surround Sound
Or, Making Beautiful
Music Together

MILEAGE: SECOND YEAR of marriage, or now.

Goal: To make friends with romance, sex and being honest with each other.

Yes, this tune-up is about sex.

Yes, I put it after _two_ years of marriage on purpose.

No, your wife hasn't been talking to me.

I can feel the panic out there. *"What! Talk about sex only every two years!!!???!!!"*

No, you don't have to wait two years to discuss sex with your wife. I put it here because you need to have *Actual Mileage* together before you make changes. You also have to develop enough trust to be honest with each other in this vulnerable area. Sex is a routine maintenance issue, but frequency of discussion depends entirely on the two of you. So does frequency of the other sort.

I put this tune-up at twenty-four months because in the first part of marriage, you don't think there's a need for understanding anything beyond the mechanics of sex. It's fun. What's there to deal with? Then routine and/ or frustration sets in. The more you talk about uncomfortable topics with each other, the easier it gets. Talk, talk, talk. Keep communication open. Learn from each other, not the media. Again, *do not* let culture make you dissatisfied with what you have. Just be honest.

Now for another shocker. You should never have sex. Sex is what people who don't care about each other have. Making love is what people who are married do. **Notice** please: you *have* sex or you *make* love. To have sex is to take. To make love is to give. One supports a life-long relationship. The other is only for the here and now. Your marriage vow was about what you promised to *give*. Married love is about giving.

Remember how I said in conflict resolution it was vital you remember the difference between compartments and wiring? Well, the same is true here. Lovemaking is all about wiring for her. If you haven't read the waffle/ spaghetti book by now, do it at this tune-up. You'll save yourself a *lot* of frustration.

For a woman, sex is wiring, which means it's influenced by <u>all</u> the other wires in her system. For you sex is a box, a big compartment, and when you go into that compartment all other compartments are irrelevant. You have access to your big compartment from *every* other compartment in your brain. She isn't wired like that. I can't emphasize this difference enough.

The reason you can be ready to go is because all you have to do is go to your favorite compartment. Everything else becomes secondary. She can't do that! Demanding sex from her without romance is just as difficult for her as demanding an erection from you when you're not in the mood. Learn to work with it instead of fighting it.

Note: One of the wires is the cultural influence on your wife's attitude toward sex, her body, and her feelings of being attractive. Women in our country never get away from being compared. You may fuss about the time and money spent on hair, make-up, getting dressed, shoes, and clothing. To a certain extent, she spends that time because she's deeply aware she's competing for your attention. It surrounds her. It's on the computer, in the grocery store, on TV, on calendars, posters, music videos, billboards, newspapers, and bumper stickers. About the only place she isn't faced with Miss Airbrushed Pert and Perky is her stores: craft shops, fabric stores, and knitting shops. The books and magazines there feature cute babies, cute hats, and cute quilts. No competition.

Try to imagine the reverse. Suddenly Home Depot and Napa are no longer bastions of male sanctuary because the moment you walk in the door you see picture after picture of guys more attractive than you. They're on the walls, the counter, the magazines, the shirts. You don't measure up. The magazines at the check-out counter are full of centerfold guys. There isn't a place you can go and not be faced with your own inadequacy, your inability to look like what journalism says is attractive. The message: you do not measure up.

Ask most women what their best feature is and they have a hard time praising anything. Ask what her worst feature is and she can go on for hours. You definitely have the power to help her rise above all that garbage. You have to tell her you find her attractive and why. Tell her often because she's assaulted often. A woman faced with the cover of Cosmo at the grocery store isn't going to feel gay abandon when it comes to sex unless you convince her she's more attractive to you and why.

You'll never understand. When someone tells you that you have great biceps, you agree. You think to yourself, *"Yeah! I'm da Man!"* You don't immediately launch into self-criticism of your abs. Be aware of the difference.

Another **Note:** She's never going to think about sex the same way you do but that doesn't mean she doesn't like it. When you tell yourself she doesn't like it, you create a problem. You look for negatives. You have a pity party. You begin to treat her with dishonor to get your needs met. Your lack of honor, encourages her to withdraw, fulfilling your prophecy. You develop bitterness and resentment, all because of something you told yourself. She didn't tell you she hates sex; you decided that for her. Stop it. You can just as easily tell yourself she likes sex and then find ways to make it true. It's a choice you make. Be a positive prophet.

Romance is the strongest tool available to you to keep her from making lists in her head during sex. Romance gets all the wires going your direction; sex alone doesn't, most of the time.

Before you married you spent hours priming her pump. The longer you're married, the less time the guy wants to spend priming the pump until time spent is almost non-existent. Then he concludes she just isn't interested anymore. I can almost guarantee if you spent even half the time you did paying attention to her during courtship, you'd find a much more interested mate. That's why dates are so important in marriage. If you've neglected this area for years, please don't expect one nice date to send her weak-kneed into your arms. She didn't fall into your arms on your first date, either. You have to warm the engine up if you've allowed it to cool off.

In a vehicle you prime the pump before you turn on the engine. How about a little romance here before you expect her to turn on for you? Those cold starts are hard on an engine and hard on a wife.

And yes, this is a two way street. She may spend less effort being attractive for you. You want to be comfortable with each other, but not so comfortable that the fire goes out. Find *your* balance.

So what exactly is romance? It's whatever you did during courtship that won her heart. A vital romance tool, no matter what make and model you have, is consideration. Expressing concern about her comfort, peace of mind, values, and goals can all be romantic. It isn't just about hearts, cards, flowers, and candy. It's more about demonstrating appreciation for her.

Music is a powerful romance tool. I'll never forget a young man I met during a summer class at the community college. He struck up a conversation and was quite animated until he saw the engagement ring on my finger. Then he decided to share his wisdom with me.

"I never hit on engaged women. They're too loyal. It's the married ones who are easier." I raised my eyebrows.

"It's so simple really. We go for a ride and talk. I turn on the music and let the tunes do all the work for me. Then..." He smiled. Actually it was more of a leer. He was probably 19. Waaaay too much knowledge without wisdom.

For heaven's sake, know her favorite music if music is her thing. Ask her. Write it down. Why do this? Because every guy wants to feel he's irresistible and music can make that happen for you! It isn't all about aftershave.

Romance honors and respects. It builds up. Romance is almost any action that says, *"I'm thinking of you. I'm focused on you. What can I do for you?"*

Why is it okay to act considerate and focused during courtship and not during marriage? Which is more important, getting married or staying married? In this instant message day, you can text her all day long telling her you're thinking of her. You already built your unique framework during courtship. Keep the connection alive.

To most guys the goal of courtship was to get the girl to say *"yes."* Once the goal is accomplished, he quits the field and moves on to other goals. Getting married is not the goal; <u>*staying*</u> married is. Repeat that line, out loud.

Women like to be loved as much as you like to be respected. That means *romance.*

Guys think sex is the same thing as romance. <u>*It isn't!*</u> Repeat this over and over. You won't understand, but you can be wise. The math is different. For you *love = sex*. Her equation is *love + romance = sex*. Sex <u>*is*</u> part of the equation. Women like sex, but in order to enjoy it, it has to be mated with romance. The level of romance depends on your model. You can do this. You romanced during courtship. You already know how because whatever you did back then revved her engine. Do it again and keep doing it.

Your tools of romance need to be more than that silly grin on your face. And, listen up here, your bag of tools needs to grow over the years. Pay attention here. You want sex? Cough up the romance. You can quit feeling sorry for yourself that you don't get it as often as you want just as soon as you start paying attention to romance.

Romance is about being together in some sense on a daily basis. That does *not* just mean sleeping under the same covers! It means conversation beyond communicating schedules. It means re-connecting after a day of being apart. To do it daily, it has to be kept simple. Flowers and candy are good in their time, but not daily. Touch. Talk. Listen. Go for a walk. Hold her. Look into her eyes. Kiss her. Do the ninety- second daily maintenance.

Note: Your wives haven't been talking to me about your sex life. All is safe. The above comments come from years of listening to guys complain about *Not Enough* and women complain about men wanting it *All The Time*. Sigh.

Sex and romance are two sides of the same gasket. You can both be happy with the investment if you take time to understand and be more concerned about her pleasure than your own. When you start meeting her needs for romance, she'll naturally turn to you. Frequency becomes a non-issue if you pay attention to romance.

Make your goal one of loving your wife extravagantly instead of cautiously.[1] Love in order to give instead of to get. If you love your wife this way, then you most likely won't have problems with sex. It's when you take more than you give that sex goes down the tubes.

Note: You have to give what *she* wants, *not* what you want to give. She's not a guy. Making love is not all about orgasm. You can't substitute orgasm for romance, I don't care how good you are.

Systems which require fine-tuning tend to get out of tune easily. The stereo is tuned with equalizers. It's a good term. If sex isn't good, check the equalizers. Are you taking more than you're giving? Find ways to balance the relationship, but make sure they're ways that are important *to her*. There's no sense in making changes she doesn't want. You can't eagerly offer your favorite thing to avoid making the change that's meaningful to her and still expect a green light.

Note: Please be sure to set your own standards here. Some couples never celebrate an anniversary and that's okay with both of them. Other couples never celebrate anything because he doesn't want to and she keeps quiet and longs for it.

You have to be honest here. Help her to be honest. You have to convince her that knowing what she really thinks is more important to you than hearing what you want to hear. This is the tune-up to get honesty established. *Without honesty you won't have good sex.* Without a commitment to honor, cherish, and respect her, you won't have good love-making. Please re-read that. I don't want you to think that if you get good at romance you can have sex any time you want it. Good love-making is about honoring each other, not about getting what you want.

Please **Note:** Spaces in intimacy don't equal spaces in love. Check your model's personality type. She may want space to re-charge her engines, not because she's withdrawing from you. To know the difference, you're going to have to ask. If you're not feeling close, then ask if you're doing anything to kill love. Always ask, *"Do we need to talk?"* Don't assume the worst just because she's quiet.

I wish we women had a noodle gauge and a romance indicator on our foreheads: the number of noodles you're up against on any given day varies. She can't tell you how many noodles are in your way. It just doesn't work like that. Her level of romance-need varies. She may be unaware of her need levels. While we don't have actual gauges, there are indicators.

One indicator of her need for romance is her interest in chick flicks and romance novels. If she's reading and watching them more than usual, you probably have a wife at least a quart low in the romance department. You need to meet her romance need, not a book or a movie. Depending on her usual levels, music can also be an indicator, especially if she's humming *"If You Don't Know Me by Now"* or some other broken heart song. Put on her favorite song. Take her in your arms and sway to the music. One song. One dance in your home. You can do this. It isn't about the dancing.

Note: Please don't confuse your legitimate need for intimacy with boredom, insecurity, fear, anger, or whatever. The desire for frequency may mask another issue. Be aware. Keep intimacy for blessing your marriage, not as a cure-all for problems you don't want to face.

Steps

Discuss the six categories below and find out her preferences. This tune-up can be done over a period of time. You don't have to learn this all at once. You just need to learn it.

1. Ask her to list her favorite Love Songs. The list will grow over the years.

Make sure you have copies of every song and make sure you play them as often as she enjoys them. Also ask for her red flag broken heart songs. These are songs she plays when she's lonely or sad. Make the list something she can add to as titles come to mind. Refer to Chapter 6.

2. Ask her to list her favorite Flowers. Women are not mechanical. That means there are times and places that flowers are appreciated and times when they are *not* appreciated. Sometimes it's roses in a vase. Sometimes it's you clutching a fistful of flowers. Other times having them delivered to her at work sets her heart throbbing. Flowers can come from the grocery store, the florist, or alongside the road. Just because it costs a lot of money doesn't guarantee her appreciation. There's a lot of room for individuality here, so use it! Don't do the same thing over and over. Think outside the box. If she loves flowers, a package of seeds or a gift certificate to a garden center may be more appreciated than a bouquet of flowers. Garden tools may be on her romance list. Ask. The more ideas she gives you, the bigger the bulls eye, the greater success you have.

3. Ask for a list of her favorite Candy. Be aware, however, candy is much more difficult to get right. You're going to have to ask how much candy is good. A pound of chocolates in a heart-shaped box may dismay her more than give her the willies. Why? It gets back to her attractiveness. If she's trying to diet, then send flowers, not candy. For the same reason, you're going to have to know how often candy is okay and when it's too much. Also, know that all chocolate is *not* created equal. Women can probably tell the difference in chocolates blindfolded just like you can beer. Also make a list for fragrances, if she wears them. Refer to Maintenance Chapter #6

4. Favorite Moves: The very moves you thought were so charming when dating may not be ones your wife thinks are charming today. You really need to ask here—remember you're thinking sex and she's thinking romance.

Guys hate those sappy chick flicks because to them they aren't about sex. News-flash—to a woman they *are* about sex! She might see you as sexy when you sit at a desk with your glasses on, doing taxes, and you won't have a clue because to you it isn't sex. How many opportunities do you really want to miss? Then ask. Ask what attracted her to you during dating. Ask what melts her heart now. Ask her to define "romance." Then please write it down and memorize it. You aren't going to understand, but you *can* know. If you don't memorize something that doesn't make sense to you, you *are* going to forget it and then end up back where you began—not getting as much as you want and blaming her for not being interested.

5. The Jewelry Box. When guys go into their box about jewelry most of them probably think *engagement ring*. That means big bucks and all the emotional tie-ins of asking someone to marry you. What a shame. Most models like jewelry and it doesn't have to be the spendy kind.

   If jewelry is romantic to her, then you need to be the one who fills that need in her. Relax. It may not be important to her at all. Some models are like that. Your wife's jewelry preferences are something you have to ask. It isn't against the rules to ask. Jewelry comes with brand names just like your underwear. Just like underwear, different stores carry different brands. You can do this. Remember, it's part of the wiring mass tied to sex. She doesn't need a different bauble every week or month, just every once in a while. It isn't against the rules to go shopping with her and have her show you her preferences. You can shop online and don't have to actually go into one of "those" stores. You can do this. You can buy it all at once, and then dole it out through-out the year. Find a way.

6. Dancing. This one is entirely model based, but you still need to ask. If dancing is her thing, then you need to learn. Period. I can't make you understand how it melts her heart. Just take it from me that it does. I have an uncle who took dance lessons to surprise his wife for their fortieth anniversary. Even after that many years of marriage, he got points—points for love, thoughtfulness, and taking the classes. Those points tallied more than the anniversary party where they actually danced. Sometimes doing the right romantic thing gets you points for a long time afterward, every time the story is told. My uncle got points galore, not only from her, but from everyone who heard about it.

The problem comes if you wait too long. The opportunity to dance may not always be there. She may have another equivalent love if dancing isn't it. Whatever it is, learn to use that tool. What you want is to build experiences into her life that she wants to tell her friends.

When Hubby proposed, he did such a good job that one of my friends wanted to hear the story over and over again. His actions built romance into our story. They were activities suited to his personality that also met my notions of romance. That's what you're going for: something that isn't out of character for you, yet meets her needs.

7. Dressing Up. This is almost a sub-category of dancing. How much, how often, and where all depend on your model. Before you groan too loudly, remember, for her it's all part of the wiring mass that leads to sex. Do you want her thinking about sex or her grocery list? If you enjoy seeing her dressed up, then buy into having to get dressed up yourself. The two of you have to match. The blessing in all this is that women remember. Give her enough romance and she'll replay over and over the times you go all out to honor her by getting all suave and debonair. Points, points, points. Do it.

The best illustration of this I can think of is a Home Improvement episode. Tim and Jill are both inclined, but timing is off, so they agree to meet later. Jill shows up all pretty. Tim shows up belching and farting after a day of watching sports and eating stadium food. It doesn't work. Jill agrees to try again. Tim shows up in work coveralls, to Jill's dismay. Tim rips off the coveralls to reveal a tuxedo. He only dressed up for a few minutes, but it did the job. Don't equate getting dressed up with an all day, tight-around-the-collar experience. You may only have to walk into the room to satisfy her need. Try it.

8. Sexy Moves. These are the character qualities that make you sexier than a flat stomach and bulging biceps. Be a good husband to your wife:

   a. *Honor her, delight in her, treat her as an equal.*[2]

   b. *Learn a life of love: love extravagantly instead of afraid of being hurt. Don't love in order to get something but to give everything of yourself.*[3]

169

    c.   *Go all out in your love for your wife—don't take advantage of her.*[4]

    d.   *Don't ever quit taking delight in her body. Never take her love for granted!*[5]

    e.   *Go all out in your love for your wife —a love marked by giving, not getting. Love to make her whole.*[6]

    f.   *Let your words evoke her beauty. Everything you do and say is designed to bring the best out of her, making her attractive.*[7]

    g.   Men like to be respected. Women like to be loved. *Do not let your love turn to lust.*[8]

9.   If you haven't read *The Five Love Languages*, do so now. There's no sense learning new tricks that don't matter to her.

10. Read "Johnny Lingo's Eight Cow Wife". You can find it on the internet. It's important and it's very short.

11. Thirty days of praise. Everyone grows more beautiful in an atmosphere of praise. Choose to think of one thing each day you appreciate about her for 30 days. Don't repeat the same things. You can do this together or on your own. One husband I know writes his wife a blog. You're free to get as creative as you want to be. It's nice to tell her in some way what you appreciate about her. Learn to think positively instead of negatively. If you choose to do this step, skip all the other steps this time. Come back and do them later.

12. Celebrate. You're doing great. I'm proud of you.

Hubby's two cents: *You aren't teaching men that romance is a panacea to get all the sex they want. Getting all the sex you want is* not *the goal; it makes your wife an object. Men need to pay more attention here because their need is so different from a woman's. If a woman decides to give the man all the intimacy he asks for, the typical man will say, "Gee, thanks," and be done. He will most likely* not *think about becoming more romantic. If, on the other hand, a man decides to meet his wife's need for romance, she most likely will become more interested in further intimacy. It's the way we're wired.*

CHAPTER 25

Tune-up #7
Ding Removal
Or, How'd That Happen?

MILEAGE: THIRD YEAR of marriage.

Goal: Ding removal.

Sometimes conflicts leave marks in the relationship. You've already worked on the initial conflict, but there's still that ding to consider. There are self-inflicted dings: branches scrape the side as you drive down a path too narrow, dropping a tailgate on a hitch, and dings from outside your control: stray shopping carts, banging car doors, getting keyed. The point is, dings happen and it's a good idea to go over them once a year to see how serious they are and what, if anything, needs to be done about them.

What do you do with a new car when you park it in a parking lot? You put it where it won't get damaged. When you come back, you inspect it carefully. You aren't checking to condemn it for getting dinged. You're checking to see if any place needs your help. Give your wife the same once-over when she's been parked in public. Inspect by asking questions and reading body language. If you notice something out of place, ask questions.

There are magical little tools for massaging out dings. The notable thing is that they don't pull. You can't restore relationship by forcing someone to return to a former way of being. Dings are worked out from the *inside*. They are massaged, not pushed.

Sometimes dealing with the ding isn't the only work necessary. Sometimes the finish needs restoration. Perfection won't happen, so work out as many dings as possible and love the rest.

What causes a ding to remain after conflict has been resolved? Family history, judging, lack of honesty, and fear are some of the causes. *Rough Roads* and *Actual Mileage* account for parking lot dings and getting keyed. The only purpose in knowing the source of the ding is to apply the correct solution, not to shift responsibility.

Ding #1: Stress Check. Parts of your relationship equate to shocks, tires, and brake pads. They're designed to absorb stresses of the road and control speed and direction. You need to annually check for wear. How's the stress of work, family, life wearing both of you down? In what areas? How can we repair that wear? What needs to be replaced?

It isn't a bad idea to take a stress test on a regular basis—maybe once a year—because stress sneaks up on you. It comes from so many small directions at once that you may be blind to the total effect. This test doesn't have to be annual, but don't let it go unchecked for more than five years. Use the test in Appendix III and date it.

An alternative is to make a list of everything that's worrying you and her and share it with each other.

One subtle agent of stress is not living in the present. What do I mean? When life gets to be too much, we tend to live in the future. *When we pay off the house, we'll…When the kids graduate, we'll…*

Living in the future is based on the assumption that you'll be able to do whatever *and* that whatever will be available for you to do. Life doesn't work like that. Once some opportunities are passed up, they're gone forever.

Living in the future is a subtle response to stress. It leads to frustration while the clock ticks. It adds up a balance due for waiting while everybody else did their thing. The rationale is we're all taking turns and her turn will come. When it doesn't, she resents others for denying her life. And if she doesn't get angry or frustrated, then one by one her dreams die and she gets flat. Take the stress test and be aware of living in the future instead of the present.

When we live too much in this mindset, we stop living in the present altogether. The present becomes something to get *through* instead of something to be alive *in*. I'm not saying don't plan. I'm just saying live in today. Once a year check for this kind of wear and see where you're living. *Don't live a life you need to get away from.*

Note: Women tend to do this more than men. Your awareness is not so much for yourself as for her. You have to know what her dreams and goals are and her plan for achieving them. You need to know how you help or hinder her plans. Ask.

Ding #2: Lack of Honesty and Fear. You *can* discuss difficult topics with your spouse. You can present different points of view, all without anger or fear. Being best friends doesn't mean absence of conflict. It means it's safe to be honest.

This chapter isn't meant to solve everyone's conflict-difficulties. Books have been written and will continue to be written on the subject. If what you read here and in the Boundaries book doesn't help, keep working at it until you find the solution that works for both of you. Deal with issues while they're small. What you don't work on accrues interest big time.

Please **Note:** Ding removal is often done by a professional. If you don't address your issues with both education and compromise, professional assistance may be necessary to remove the dings of bitterness, resentment, and critical attitudes.

Note: It can't work for just you. You're a partnership. If it doesn't work for both then it doesn't, in fact, work for either of you. You can't say *"Hey! After I vent, I'm fine. My anger is just who I am and shouldn't bother anyone else."* That's an escape from responsibility. Don't go there.

Ding #3: Family Dynamics. In effect we all live in second marriages. Your parent's marriage is your first marriage. You carry expectations and baggage from it. None of us came from the factory without a few blems. The trick is being able to identify when she's mad at all men because of something dad did, and when she's legitimately mad at you for something *you* did. Add to this mix personality and life experiences and we bring home a lot of stuff and want our mate to pay for it. Sort it out.

Look at your own heritage. Actively choose to make changes. You can respond to a lousy family history in two opposite ways. One way reasons, "*I had a lousy childhood. Life isn't fair. My kids have to learn to be tough the same as I did. That's the reality of life.*"

Another way reasons, "*I had a lousy childhood. I want my kids to have it better than I did. I'm going to learn different tools of marriage so I don't pass on what I inherited. Life isn't fair, but in my own home I will choose healthy ways of living with my family.*"

How you handle conflict today should be different from how you handle it ten years from now. Developing conflict resolution skills is one of your goals. In order to grow, you have to look at how your family handled conflict, what you took away from that style, and where you want it to be different or the same.

Dings have to do with staying mad. Part of the problem for her is all those wires. One of those wires is about protection. Being the bigger and stronger of the two of you, protection usually falls to the male. That doesn't mean she can't or won't do it. But I've heard men say their wives got hard. What they missed was that the wife faced hard situations without his protection. You can't live your life free of responsibility and expect her to remain gentle.

Yes, there's balance here. Male protection is not an excuse for female immaturity. You're not supposed to be a monster, she's not supposed to be a ditz. The point is, the protection issue comes out in ways you don't recognize. She gets home first and waits for you to come home. While waiting for you, she assumes your protector role. When you don't call or show up when expected, part of the reason she stresses is because she's filling your role of protector. She expects her shift to end. When her replacement doesn't show up, she's both worried about you *and* filling your role. Ding, ding.

The best reversal I can think of happens when women go off to a weekend conference, leaving the man at home to fill *her* role. It's incredible how many men call to check on the wife; how many children are put on the phone to tell mommy how much they all miss her, and all this happens in the first two hours of the three-day conference! If the woman calls the man while he's at a conference, she's seen as clingy.

The biggest difference between the male being left with female responsibilities and the female left with male responsibilities is that the male gets help. Males call up a babysitter to deal with poopy diapers and pizza delivery to take care of hunger pangs. It's tough for a female to call in another male to make her feel safe.

Ding #4: Judging. This is both good and bad. When you hear *should* and *ought,* judging is happening. When you feel self-righteous, judging is happening. Saying there aren't any rules isn't the answer, either. Try driving down the road with no rules.

Judgment doesn't equal right or wrong or even truth. Why not? Groups form their own rules.

In our travels we've noticed in some communities everyone tends to run red lights. We can feel quite virtuous until we realize that when those same roads are covered with ice and snow seven months of the year, braking for a red light requires less rigidity about rules and more awareness of actual driving conditions. All the smug, superior judging of those people is hollow. What makes no sense to us, visiting during the summer, makes perfect sense during their winter, which lasts most of the year! Stopping at red lights is a darn good idea, but it has to be applied with wisdom. The same is true of judgment. It's the critical spirit behind the judgment that's wrong, not the judgment itself.

Another problem with judgment is that it always brings you to a frustrated place of enforcement. Let me say it again, *judgment always brings you to a place of frustrated enforcement.* You decide right and wrong, but have no way of imposing your will on the world around you. The more judgmental you are, the more frustrated you become.

When we don't apply reason to rules we end up defending principles while the road slips out from under us. *Clinging to the way you think life ought to be may mean you end up with a principle instead of a marriage.*

Note: A discussion becomes a disagreement when the goal changes. The goal of a discussion is to find the best way to go the same direction. The goal of a disagreement is to be right. Remember, you're on the same team.

Note: Sometimes someone has to be right. Sometimes it's her and sometimes it's you. I come back to the definition of love: *"Love is gentle, kind, patient. Love doesn't keep a record of wrongs. Love rejoices in the truth. Love is not rude, self-seeking or easily angered. Love always trusts, protects, hopes, and perseveres. Love doesn't envy, isn't proud, and doesn't boast."*[1] If what you're doing or feeling during a conflict doesn't match up with this definition, then acknowledge it right away.

You can be right in your point and wrong in your motives. Wrong motives defeat you every time, whether you're right *or* wrong. Confess where you're wrong and *then* discuss the topic at hand.

Note: There's a difference between celebrating truth and celebrating being right. One focuses on God and the other focuses on self.

Beware of demanding your rights without also taking your full measure of responsibility. Don't listen to our culture which emphasizes rights over responsibility. Demanding your rights produces a sense of entitlement and an aura of victimization. You won't do a good job "spousing" or parenting if you're focused on your rights. Your wedding vows were about giving, not what you're owed.

Knowing your rights is great, but the minute you make someone else responsible for them, you give away your autonomy. The power to live a fruitful life comes from taking responsibility,[2] not from demanding someone else do whatever for you.

This becomes a ding when she feels forced into doing something she didn't want to do. Sometimes you push too much. Sometimes she doesn't take responsibility to hold her boundaries. Everybody needs to grow. If you hear something like, "*I really didn't want to do this and you made me,*" apologize. Then ask, "*How can I help you tell me, 'No?' How can I tell the difference between a fearful reaction and thought-out preference?*"

And that brings us to the inevitable—being wrong. When you started driving, you began with a bike. Falling off a bike meant skinned knees and hands. You limped home and had Mom assess the damage and choose the appropriate course of action. It's the same with relationship. If the disagreement involved gravel imbedded, then, no matter how painful, it has to be removed and treated for infection. Ignoring it will not make it go away. It only festers. We used to use *lots* of hydrogen peroxide. Find something that's as painless to bubble out the seeds of infection in your relationship.

Ding #5: Rough Roads/Actual Mileage. Planning for hard times helps diminish the number of dings. You have to have experienced a few rough roads in order to know how to plan for them. Your plans won't cover all your bases, but you'll have talked through what you imagine you'll do if such and such happens. Your plans need to be general so they apply to a variety of circumstances. This is where your strengths and weaknesses need to be discussed openly. In order for love to cover weakness, weakness has to be revealed.

Steps:

1. Set aside time for this tune-up. Massaging dings takes time.

2. Books to read and discuss: *Boundaries for Marriage, The Language of Apology,* and *Money Before Marriage* (See Appendix II). Choose one. You need to do all three, but for now just do the one that seems the most relevant. Do the other two at a later tune-up. Learn about each other. Value your differences.

3. Do a self-inflicted ding assessment. Rate yourselves and each other on your family history, judgmentalism, lack of honesty, fears. Finding out what the old dings are isn't the goal. Find out why they're still there and what it takes to ease them out of your relationship. Ding

removal often has to be done by a professional, but that doesn't mean the counselor's couch. Consider a book specific to your needs. If that doesn't work, then go see a flesh-and-blood professional.

4. Do an *Actual Mileage/Rough Road* ding assessment. What is work doing to your marriage? What are outside activities doing to your marriage? What are children doing to your marriage?

5. Discuss your strengths and weaknesses in relation to conflict. Promise to cover weakness with love. Define what that means to each of you. Write it down.

6. Establish boundaries and apology phrases. Write them down. Memorize them.

7. Do the stress test in Appendix III.

8. Discuss how much you tend to live in the future. Find out why.

9. Celebrate.

CHAPTER 26

Tune-up #8
Some Assembly Required
Or, Putting the Pieces Back Together

MILEAGE: THIRD YEAR of marriage, annually hereafter.

Goal: Putting the Pieces Back Together: forgiveness.

Tune-ups mean two things—taking something apart *and* putting it back together. This tune-up is about putting your relationship back together. It requires new attitudes, new skills. You don't tear down an engine and put it back together with old parts. Forgiveness and repentance are the new parts. If you tore down an engine and then put the old parts back, you'd still have the same problem because, even though you diagnosed the problem, you didn't change anything to *fix* the problem. Agreeing that something is a problem won't solve it. You need to learn to say, "*I'm sorry. I was wrong. I'll change.*"

In order to repair an engine, you have to identify the part numbers, use appropriate tools, and follow prescribed steps. What to replace and when is a matter of opinion. There's wisdom in *If It Ain't Broke, Don't Fix It.* There's also wisdom in being proactive and not waiting for things to break. The point is, usually there are warning signs when something is going to break. One broken thing often breaks something else, so it's best to be proactive.

For instance, windshields crack—sometimes you know the exact moment

179

the rock came flying at you. Other times the light hits that tiny speck just right and you know you have a chip. If you take care of it right away, then you've saved the windshield. If you ignore it, then the crack grows and you need to replace the glass. The same principle holds here—ignore the problem and it grows bigger and costs more to repair.

You can't have love without forgiveness. Most often you can't forgive unless you've been forgiven. To be good at forgiveness, you have to have actual miles under your belt. You have to look in the face of the long ago Bride and see tears and hurt that you caused, and then own it. In other words, you have to have failed. Out of failure comes willingness to forgive and the humility to ask for and give forgiveness.

It isn't a matter of just forgetting deep hurts. It's a matter of, in God's vernacular, choosing to remember no more.[1] It's a choice we make and we really make it for ourselves. Forgiving frees us from other people and from the past. Jesus said, *"You're asking the wrong question. You're looking for someone to blame. Look instead for what God can do."*[2]

Forgiving requires us to change our focus. It can be very hard work. Let's look at tools, parts necessary for success, and steps required.

Tool #1: Personality. Your personality type is both your strength and your weakness. What you need for successful conflict resolution comes from your personality.

For example, I hate debating. I need to discuss, ponder, discuss. In conflict then, I have to have several times of conversation with periods of reflection in between. To discuss a topic and not be able to re-visit it frustrates me, so part of my conflict resolution includes permission to keep bringing up the topic until we're talked out. I treasure Hubby because when he notices A Mood, he asks, *"Do we need to talk?"* The more often he asks, the more confident I become and the less often he has to ask. You two help each other in the same way.

The strength of my personality is that I'm tolerant and don't anger easily. The weakness is that my tolerance can become avoidance when there's an issue to be faced. Since I don't like conflict, if you yell or demand an immediate answer, I'll tell you what you want to hear instead of what you're asking, just to get rid of you. It isn't honest and it just means we'll have to deal with the same problem again and again.

Even though I want you to treat me differently, I can't control you. I need to take responsibility for myself. *"I know you're really upset, but as long as you're yelling, I can't discuss the problem. When you're done yelling, let me know and I'll be willing to work on the issue."*

The point is you have to know yourselves well enough to tell each other what you need in conflict. Tell each other what makes you afraid, your weakness. Promise to help each other.

Think of the windshield here. Both sides have to be addressed in order for the two of you to travel safely. You can scrape all the ice off the outside and still be unable to see through the fog on the inside. Learn to take care of both ways of looking at the road. Allow two different approaches to both be right.

This brings up the issue of living in the present again—a very necessary skill. We tend to live in the past or the future. To be really present *in* the present is an art. Cultivate it. It means listening instead of planning what you're going to say next. It means addressing the issue today instead of hoping it'll just go away. Quit telling yourself that *when this happens, then I will _____.* Delayed dreams aren't good. You have no guarantee that any of the same elements will be present in the future. This takes us back to goals—define the goals of today. List the tasks necessary to achieve those goals and then start working on them.

Tool #2: Gender. We're back to the wires and components here. Forgiveness for you means one issue. For her, forgiveness means everything connected to the wire. She doesn't remember all the nuances to gain power over you. She remembers because that's the way she's wired. Yes, you need to deal with one issue at a time, but allow for the wiring factor. She gets just as frustrated with you because you can't see the big picture as you get frustrated with her because she can't stick to one point. Make the difference your strength instead of using it against each other. You need to ask, *"What am I not seeing?"* She needs to ask, *"Where am I losing focus here?"*

181

Tool #3: A Room of Her Own. It isn't 100 percent, but more than likely your woman would like a private space. When she has a place to relax, she won't be as stressed. If she isn't as stressed, you'll have fewer conflicts. It doesn't have to be 10' x 20'. My first room was a walk-in closet. I loved it. Kind of like Terry Bradshaw's naked room in *Failure to Launch*, except she doesn't want a room to be naked in. She wants a place to retreat to. It'll be the one place in the house that lowers her blood pressure at the end of her day.

Did you know that a guy's blood pressure generally drops when he gets home? A woman's generally goes up. That's not good. She is *"on"* all day at work. When she comes home, she's tired *and* *"on"* until she goes to bed. This isn't whining. It's the way things are. There's no right or wrong on after-work issues. Don't let culture make either of you unhappy if what you're doing works for both of you. Make certain, however, that *both* of you are happy.

I hear you say, *"But the whole house is hers!"* Really? Does she have as much autonomy over the house as you do over the shop? Does she tell everyone in the house what tools they may/may not use, when and how they have to be treated or they will lose the privilege of use? Probably not. In the house the rules are usually by consensus, not hers alone. Ask her what a space of her own would look like and then make it happen. It'll save you conflicts because she has a place to decompress instead of on you.

Note: This is a reminder. We've covered it before, but guys forget. Women tend to say *"Okay"* when they mean much more. *"Okay"* can mean, *"I'll do it this time."* or *"I'll go along for now, but next time it's my turn."* or something else. The point is, *"Okay"* doesn't necessarily mean she's in total agreement with the situation. How do you know what her *"Okay"* means? Ask. Ask, *"Is this 'Okay' really okay, or is there more I need to know?"*

Girls, if he asks, then give him the honest answer in a polite tone of voice. He wants to know you better so let him do so. Also, when the guy realizes that he's entering a transaction instead of getting unconditional agreement, he may look for a more mutual option.

Tool #4: Trust. Trust is like a credit card. You begin your relationship with a certain credit limit. Conflict damages your credit. Marriages don't break down because of conflict alone. They break down because of *unresolved* conflict—a very important distinction. Focus on the right issue in order to solve it.

If you abuse your trust limit too often, pretty soon you may still be married and yet have a zero credit limit. Fortunately, it isn't necessarily irreparable. This is assuming that both of you want to make this work. Nobody can make it work alone.

You can build trust up again, but it's a long, slow process and someone else determines when you've earned a new rating. You don't tell the credit bureau when you've done all you want to do that they ought to give you the rating you desire. When you've broken trust in your marriage, you pay the price for a long time until *she's* satisfied.

You either build relationship or you wear it down. You'll do both by the way you handle conflict. The vital lesson is learning *how* to deal with broken trust. When you were in high school, my goal was to teach you how to fail. I knew that once you left home you'd make many mistakes, just like I did. I wanted you to learn that *failing doesn't make you a failure.* Failing is just a step in learning. Learning *how* to overcome is the key to learning how to recover trust. Ask. Figure out what you need to know in order to establish trust as a core value of your relationship. Work toward being able to speak up without fear of rejection, abandonment, or punishment.

Learning how to fall is a key to not getting hurt in martial arts. It takes practice. The same principle holds true in marriage. You will fall. Practice learning how.

After a tiff, it's always wise to ask, *"Do you still trust me?"* You each have to be honest and not try to get revenge or manipulate. Honesty, honesty, honesty even if you gag on it.

You need to find out *why* trust broke down. Was it the pollution around you, a fender-bender, a factory blem, old history, or present Stuff? If trust has been broken, then ask how it can be restored again and then do it. Ask, *"What do you need to hear?"* Apologize. Re-state the goals and values of your marriage. *"I want our relationship based on mutual love and respect. I've broken it. Please forgive me."*

WARNING: Do *not* say, *"I'll try to do better."* "Try" means you aren't serious. Instead agree on a process. *"The next time I blow it, I will _____. If you see me doing _____, will you help me and say _____ so I don't get so stuck in my ways?"*

One of the best gifts Hubby gave me was permission. He told me, *"Don't let me get away with _____."* I believed him and so I don't. Sometimes he feels like he's created a monster; other times he's thankful. Either way, it keeps us healthy because we're valuing honesty. He holds me accountable as well. It has to work both ways. We're all blind to our own faults. We all need someone we trust to tell us when we're out of line. How much better to have someone who loves us tell us rather than the jerk at work who could care less. Being honest protects the marriage. Value it highly.

Tool #5: Boundaries. If you haven't read one of the *Boundaries* books by now, this is a good time.

Crossing someone's boundaries causes conflict. The problem is, not all boundaries are visible. Some are like the hidden fences for dogs. Unless there's good communication, you may not know a boundary is even there until you've been shocked, picked yourself up off the ground, and wondered, *"What hit me?"* Nothing was visible until you crossed the line, buried underground, and then, SNAP! You got it.

We all have boundaries. They're healthy. They define where our differences are. They flex. Visible or not, when they're broken, in order to feel safe again, we set a boundary of distance between us. Boundaries aren't always communicated clearly, hence the need for a tune-up where you do communicate as many as you're aware of. Also agree to give each other grace when you crash into a boundary that wasn't communicated. You'll need to do this all your married life because boundaries change. Practice taking those falls.

Boundaries aren't a set-in-stone thing. To set boundaries at all implies continued relationship and is an offer of future relationship. Boundaries say, *"If you can regain my trust, I'll move the boundary closer and let you be close to me again, even though you broke my trust."* See boundaries as positive and work on them seriously. They say, *"This is how we're different; this is how we're the same."*

CAUTION: If you're not committed to the relationship, it'll come out during conflict. If in the back of your mind divorce is always an option, you won't find the solution you need. If divorce isn't an option, you'll keep at a problem until a solution develops.

There's a difference between marriage experience and marriage success. Both types of marriages can last a long time. If you're going to seek mentors, find those who succeed, not those who endure.

Tool #6: Make a Do-Over Calendar. To me there are lots of starting-over places during a year. January is obvious—it's a new year. Time to start over. June is a new season—it's the end of school and the beginning of summer. September is the end of summer, the beginning of a new school year. December is Advent. Spring is Lent. A meteor shower is just as valid of an excuse for a new beginning. Give yourself lots of them. All they are is permission to do-over. The more places for do-overs you program into your relationship, the more room you give it to grow and stay healthy. Make your own calendar. Add a promise that either one of you can ask for a do-over at any time, or every Thursday or every tenth of the month. Be as random and as flexible as you want to be. Just be sure to do it.

Tool #7: Listening. You can become polarized during conflict when both of you are hurting. Apologies aren't sincere because the hurt outweighs the heart for the moment. The sealed engine blows a seal, a piston or valves. New gaskets—apologies—can be applied and still not seat. An apology can be given and still not heal the relationship because small bits of detail corrupt the smooth surface necessary for a complete seal.

To achieve proper working order, go through the *Language of Apology* (See Appendix II). Look at the examples at the end of each chapter and keep trying them until you find one that dissolves the gunk and re-seats the gasket. Look over the list of lubricants in the Maintenance section and use the appropriate one. Once you've cleaned the interface between the two of you, don't keep pulling at it. Let it go and move on.

Note: Please be honest here. Do *not* say the words so you feel good. Say the words to heal the hurt you caused. Care more about the effect of your words than about being right. This comes right back to goals.

Listen to your words during conflict. Diversions such as *What about you!? You do the same thing!* are attempts to avoid the issue at hand. Whenever you hear blame words, know that someone is trying to avoid responsibility. The point may be true—the other person might do the very thing they're nailing you for doing. Solve one issue at a time. Don't stuff your opinion, just deal with it when it isn't an attempt to get responsibility for your behavior on someone else's back.

If you hear the *"Did-not, did-too"* argument, you need to stop and ask yourself why you need to be right. Is fear part of the problem? What are you afraid of? You need to turn mentally from getting what you want toward solving the problem. Ask her to help you understand her point of view and then *listen*. Listen to the words and listen even more carefully to their meaning. This is where you use the Pink Hearing Aid. Try to follow her wiring. Ask her to translate wiring into components. Make it work for both of you.

Listen to your words. If you find recurring patterns in your conflicts—and who of us doesn't—then spend some time looking at the common thread. If you feel the entire world is just too sensitive and you have to walk on eggshells around everybody, then take time to see if you're the one being insensitive and the eggshells are actually bunkers of self-protection against you.

If you see the same pattern with one person after another, then you're likely driving the same route. Get new map coordinates. Change the route you're taking. You can spend a lifetime fighting about taking the garbage out and garbage is never the issue. It can take real work to get to the heart of the matter, but if you don't do it, your marriage engine will always sputter and lose power when you need it most.

Listen to your words. The phrase, *"at my expense"* comes to mind. If the way you live—whether it's how you spend time, money, or entertain yourself—is *at her expense*, then you owe a debt every time you charge on her account. If you're at a party, and just can't resist making fun of her for not getting the checkbook balanced, that's *at her expense* and you owe her a debt. If you commit to dinner with her and then fail to show up, that's *at her expense* and you owe her. She's paying for your irresponsibility.

Standing on someone else's back doesn't make you look tall. If the laughter, criticism, or broken promise has been public and *at-her-expense* has cost her reputation, then you need to restore her reputation just as publicly. Yes, it's humiliating. And yes, it's necessary. Do it once or twice and you'll find those comments aren't quite so much fun to make. You'll also have a more trusting relationship.

Tool #8: Forgive. The other part of making mistakes and being wrong is asking forgiveness. Not just, *"I'm sorry."* But also, *"Will you forgive me?"* In a sense, forgiveness belongs at the very beginning of this discussion because without it you won't go anywhere.

With deep hurts, forgiveness feels too much like letting the other person off the hook and can be nearly impossible to do. Deep hurts are more than gravel under the skin. They're broken bones and internal bleeding. They require much more than a Band-Aid. This is where God's role in your relationship is critical. He's the one you must trust for justice when life is unjust; when the hurt can't be healed with flowers or candy; when the injury has changed your relationship forever. Good *can* come of it, but by refusing to forgive, *you're* the one stuck. Stuck in the past. The day was new, but you choose to live in the past remembering yesterday's pain.

Living in the past is just as bad as living in the future. By forgiving, you let *yourself* go from an event in the past and choose to move on. You allow the event to make you stronger instead of bitter. It is a choice *you* make.

Note: I'm *not* advocating denial of painful events. Forgiving comes after you've attempted to work things through with another person. Whether or not the result was satisfactory, and *especially* if not, forgiveness lets you move on.

Note: Confronting painful events means commitment to follow through. You're probably not the one to confront if you're not *also* willing to help heal the hurt. If you tear down the engine, put it back together.

Tool #9: Budget Time. You can't spend all your energy away from home and expect a quality marriage. Learn to say "no" to work, projects, hobbies, sports, volunteering, to whatever uses up the energy you need for the most important relationship in your life apart from your faith. Come home with enough energy left to give. Time is one aspect of life where none of us is richer than another. We all have twenty-four hours to spend. Spend time on your marriage to have a healthy one.

Steps:

1. 1. During non-crisis times go through one of the books together: *Language of Apology* and *Boundaries For Marriage*. Think of unresolved conflicts and pick out what you needed to hear. Have her do the same then trade lists and discuss them. Remember this is a tune-up—it takes time and it's necessary. It's taking apart *and* putting back together. Keep the list in front of you—not the list of hurts but the list of what she needs to hear. Think of the words as replacement part numbers. It's her language. If you want to succeed at resolving conflicts with her, you <u>have</u> to know the proper part number to apply.

2. Discuss what *A Room of Her Own* looks like to her, or if it's even an issue. Allow her to dream as big as you like to dream about shops, sports, tools, etc. Then find a way to give her space in the reality of today, just as your shop is your reality. That wonderful studio may be years away, but her need of refreshing space is now. Don't think too literally here. *A Room of Her Own* may mean she has simply has time to herself to go for a walk, run, shopping, or whatever fills her up.

3. Review personality from the aspect of conflict resolution. Share strengths and weaknesses. Look at the DISC chart in Appendix III and review what you each need in each other, your values, and favorite sayings.

4. Discuss issues of trust. Ask: *"Where do you know you can count on me? Where do you know I'm probably not going to follow through? Where have I broken your trust and what will it take to re-build it?"* Review your marriage goal at the beginning and end of this discussion.

5. Share with each other what your Rules of Life are. Share with each other what boundaries bit you. Unexposed boundaries are like frayed wiring—get too close and you're going to get hurt. Work together to communicate as many boundaries are you're aware of. Update your definition often.

6. Discuss mentors. There's a big difference between marriage experience and marriage success. Both types of marriages can last a long time. Find mentors who succeed, not those who endure. And always listen with discernment. There's an old proverb: *"Can a blind man guide a blind man? Wouldn't they both end up in the ditch? An apprentice doesn't lecture the master. The point is to be careful who you follow as your teacher."*[3]

7. Make up a Do-Over Calendar or at least a do-over attitude. Agree that when one of you wants another chance, it can happen. Discuss what it'll take to have second chances.

8. Discuss what you hear during conflict. Discuss the word, *"Okay."* Discuss blame words, and *at-my-expense* words, and Pink Hearing Aids. Discuss conflicts that repeat. If after a number of years you're still repeating the same type of conflict, it may mean there's an issue of forgiveness to be resolved. You may need to forgive yourself for being imperfect, others for betrayal, or immaturity. Don't continue to live with these conflicts. Look for the seed, weed it out, and move on. Every choice you make either advances you toward your goal or away from it. Choose wisely.

9. Celebrate.

CHAPTER 27

Tune-up #9
Seat Belts Required
Or, Parenting

MILEAGE: BEFORE THE baby arrives and every three months after birth for the first year. If all goes well, then annually.

Goal: To establish yourselves as parenting partners. This chapter isn't about parenting; it's about how to understand your wife as parent.

The purpose of a tune-up is to check. It's a preventive measure. If you check, you spot potential problems before they become real problems. If you've been doing all the other tune-ups before you became parents, this tune-up is easier. You're already a unit. You already know and understand each other. You're ready for the next challenge of being parents.

To begin as sexual partners and parents before you've done the basic work of building relationship is like building the walls of the house without putting down a foundation. The foundation is still necessary, but now you have to figure out how to support the structure you've built while also building a foundation. It's do-able, just much more difficult. Hang in there.

Even if this is the first time you've walked down the aisle, this is still your second marriage. Why? Because, no matter how far away you move, you're still a product of your parent's marriage. Your marriage style reflects the way your parents treated each other. Your parenting style reflects the way they treated you. It's worth a good long look.

The first time you do this tune-up, it's important to actually take the covers off your marriage engine, starter, air filter, etc. to see what things look like beneath the surface. You don't do a tune-up on a vehicle and never take things apart, do you? It's just as silly to do a marriage tune-up without getting to the heart of matters. You're setting aside time to do this, so do it thoroughly, even though it looks like touchy-feely stuff.

Your first parenting tune-up will be very different from later ones. I smile as I write this because everyone starts out strong on theory and light on application. It's funny how those bold, and usually loud, public statements about "*MY children won't*" this-or-that aren't heard after a few months of reality. And you *never* hear them after the first child.

A place to start this check-up is with parenting styles. Everyone wants to be a good parent and everyone falls short of the mark. Choose to improve on what you were given. Our family overcomes. Carry on that tradition in marriage and parenting.

What you grew up with wasn't perfect. Forgive and move on. We all had to. Forgiveness sets you free from the past. I started asking you to forgive me when you were an infant. I realized I was going to make a lot of mistakes and the innocent one in my arms was going to pay for them. If you practice asking your children's forgiveness while they're little, it becomes so much easier when they're bigger. It also sets an example for them to follow.

Parenting styles can be reduced to three types.

1. Permissive Parents are just that, permissive. These parents think that by not having rules or discipline the child will grow up happy and free. There are no boundaries, no rules, and no consistency. Unfortunately, children of this style grow up fearful.

2. Authoritarian Parents go to the other extreme. Life is all about rules and punishment. These children also grow up afraid.

3. Authoritative Parents are a blend of the two. They don't abdicate their

parental authority, nor do they act like dictators. Their children know the difference between discipline and punishment. Rules are present, clear, and consistently communicated with loving enforcement. Children grow up confident and secure.

Start this tune-up by looking over your mileage logs. How were you raised? Determine the patterns that worked for you and those that didn't work. Discuss how you're going to do things differently. Then remember that you're just beginning. Some of your ideas won't work because they're not such good ideas after all. Some of them won't work because they aren't right for that particular child. Stay teachable.

We teach so others can learn self-discipline. We don't have to teach if we intend to force others into obedience. You'll quickly find it's far easier to pick up after a toddler than it is to teach him to pick up. But, if the toddler hasn't been taught to pick up after herself, the teenager certainly won't. And the adult child won't. And your child as an adult parent still won't. It'll break your heart. Teach the toddler to pick up.

Programming the GPS: Goals.

By the time children come along, hopefully you've become practiced at making wise goals. Is the goal of raising children to make them mind? To have well-behaved children? To help the child to behave? If the goal is to make the child mind, then the two of you will be locked into a duel. He'll misbehave, waiting for you to make him behave—authoritarian parenting. How exhausting.

If the goal is to help the child behave, then he learns to behave because it's *his* choice, not because an external force demands it of him.

When I was teaching you to drive, I got into the habit of "applying" the imaginary brakes and accelerator on the passenger side of the car. I tried to let you make the decisions, but I was reacting to traffic situations with my body language. Since we lived on a highway, there were lots of moments of panicked instruction: "NO! STOP! GOOOOO!" Years later you confessed that you didn't bother reading traffic for yourself. You knew

I'd be signaling some choice. You waited until you saw me react and then did what was required. Somehow, I'd communicated that you needed to trust my judgment more than develop your own. It wasn't at all what I'd intended, but the fruit was there to see.

Find out what *you're* communicating without intending to. Check the fruit of your parenting. Preschool children are incredibly accurate mirrors. Fortunately the fruit will change if *you* change the seed you're sowing.

I thought I was being a good parent until you asked to do something one day. I opened my mouth to reply, but before I said a word, you were repeating your request, *"But, Mom..."* Your mirror showed I was saying *"no"* too often. I needed to change.

Parents get frustrated because their child doesn't respond when they call. Check the mirror. When the child calls the parent, does the parent ignore them? We think we're teaching them to be patient by making them wait, but what they're learning is to ignore people when they want your attention.

Consequences and consistency are more important than punishment.

Parenting isn't a battle unless you make it one. Anger isn't a good tool. Anger produces all sorts of wrong goals—at the top of the list is people-pleasing at the expense of honesty. Disciple, don't punish. Teach responsibility and give responsibility and you won't have rebellion.

Family is great, but one of the worst things you can do is to tell a child he's just like so-and-so. Self-fulfilling prophecy is huge with children and it covers over—sometimes to the point of obliteration—their own unique potential.

If you tell a child he *is* bad, he'll fulfill that expectation. If you tell him he doesn't mind, then he won't mind. Separate his actions from his character. Tell him that what he *did* was wrong and why. Show him the consequences. Be the discipler alongside in the discipline process instead of the punisher with arms folded over chest looking sternly apart and down on them.

We're still discussing goals. If the goal is to make the child mind, there's a *reason* for the goal. The child must mind because…out of control children embarrass me, or I want to be admired for having obedient children, or whatever. The point is, such a goal is about the *parent*, not the child. Children know this and rebel. We have to come out of our emotional need and learn instead to minister to *their* need.

When the goal is to help the child mind, then actions and words will be discipling instead of coercive. The child will know he's being helped instead of being forced. He may not like it, but he'll accept it better.

When you force others to comply, one of the many things you communicate is you believe your appeal to goodness in them will fail. Your actions say that "unless others are forced by me to do what is '*right*', or '*good*', then '*good*' simply won't happen." It should come as no surprise when our children reflect that belief. Coercive obedience only works as long as you're there to enforce it. Discipled behavior carries on when you're not there. Guess which one is easier.

Don't let issues of discipline—taking out the garbage, doing laundry, brushing teeth, doing dishes—*become* the issue so that when the child grows up they refuse to do the chores because of you.

Making a child behave doesn't yield a healthy child. It equals rebellion. Teaching says, "*This is what the child needs to know/be/like/do to be successful and I will guide him to valuing that behavior.*" Forcing him builds a bond between you. It says, "*You aren't able to learn and I have to be there to make you.*" It can last well into adulthood and ends only when the child confronts his rebellion and chooses virtue for its own sake.

Once again, it's a lot easier to pick up the toys yourself rather than teach them the responsibility and self-discipline of taking care of their possessions. If you pick up after them, they'll always expect someone to pick up after them. You can't have it both ways.

Teaching children to pick up their toys is more work than doing it yourself. An undisciplined parent can't disciple a child. You can't scream at the GPS for not going where you wanted to go if you're not willing to learn how to program the GPS.

When I hear a parent complain, "*I can't get my child to do* _____." a red flag goes up. Are they trying to force the child to be like themselves or encourage the child to be herself? A child who resists piccolo lessons may not be rebelling as much as trying to say piccolo isn't his thing.

One of the purposes of childhood is to explore their world. Too many parental demands to follow through on every attempted activity will soon produce a child who won't try *any* new activity—not because they lack interest, but because they resist being forced to follow through on something she tried and didn't like.

Make plenty of room for mistakes. Mistakes are a necessary part of the learning process, not an indicator of failure or value. If you're a perfectionist, don't pass it on. Quality is great, but not to the point where children won't try because they're afraid of getting "*it*" wrong.

I love the story about Thomas Edison's mother in your Value Tales. One day Edison spilled milk on the floor. He and his mother looked at the mess. She could tell he wanted to explore so instead of yelling she gave permission. She figured it was already a mess so why not let him learn about it? Her permission encouraged him to explore his world freely. Think about parenting every time you turn on Edison's light bulb.

Another possible reason for the child who isn't doing what the parent wants is the parent not wanting to make the effort to teach the child. Remember, I had to teach you what "*listen*" meant before I could ask you to do it.

This also brings to mind the parent who criticizes the child to others in front of the child. When children are infants, we get in the habit of talking about them in front of them. It isn't a healthy habit for many reasons, such as: One, children follow your model. If you criticize them, they'll learn to criticize you in front of others. Two, children are literal. When you talk about the problems of being a parent, they tend to think *they're* the problem. When they hear you talk about difficulty in pregnancy, or nursing, or being an at-home parent, they think *they're* responsible. They're little and can't do a thing about your problems except feel bad about themselves, maybe for the rest of their lives.

Guard carefully your conversation around little ones. They understand more than you think. You may do more damage than you realize.

Define your parenting goal well. If you want to do a good job, you need to define *"good job"* just like you had to define *"good marriage."* The GPS doesn't know what *"on vacation"* means unless you define a destination.

A *"good job"* may mean they didn't get into trouble, graduated, and we're still speaking. Or it may mean helping them discover their own potential. To settle for, *"they didn't get in trouble"* is setting the bar pretty low.

I think of a garden here. *"They didn't get in trouble"* is like keeping a garden weeded. Nothing bad grows there, but neither does anything good. There's no fruit. It's just weed-free. You have to invest yourself in helping children pursue their interests. In order for them to discover their interests, you have to give them unconditional exposure to lots of different experiences. The sooner you get them on the road to pursuing their interests, the less trouble they get into.

Note: The interests have to be *theirs*—not what *you* want them to like. Parenting is self sacrificing, just like marriage. You have to deal with your past. Don't make the child do what you regret not doing. Neither do you make the child do what *you* do because you want them to be like you. Help the child discover who *he* is and then help him grow in the direction he's bent.

Note: They have to fit into *their* culture. Your ways fit into your culture. If you label everything they do differently as wrong, they'll have trouble. Different isn't necessarily wrong.

Sometimes Authoritarian Parenting comes from a sense of entitlement. Demanding my rights, especially from a child, doesn't translate into great parenting. A strong sense of entitlement won't produce either a good marriage or good parenting. It's more about your rights than about your responsibilities. Focus instead on what you can give to the relationship.

As either a parent or a spouse, if you want to successfully lead, then you have to serve those who follow you.[1] *It isn't about you.*

Parenting gets back to commitment. If I have personal goals and I want help achieving then, then buy the help or find like-minded individuals who also want that goal. In a family, however, you're part of a whole, not *the* whole. When your goals cause others to sacrifice, it takes away from them and therefore from the whole to which you belong. If *your* goals take from *them*, you have an obligation to serve them until they accomplish *their* goals. It can't be all about you and your goals, even if your goal is to provide for your family. People willingly follow to be taken care of, not to become slaves to your desires.

I love the story of a day in the life of King David[2]. He began his day with a celebration—dancing, singing, making presentations, worshipping, blessing others, giving gifts, delegating authority, establishing new traditions, explaining, demonstrating, and assigning responsibilities and chains of command, finishing, and sending people home. A pretty busy day. *"And David went home to bless his family."*[3] When you come home from work, your goal is to bless your family.

Sealants

I'm so blessed that the style of male parenting has changed. I applaud your generation for being much more involved than past generations of men have been. Keep it up. You've found the magic sealant.

When a woman gives birth to a baby, a flood of oxytocin releases into her system. That chemical helps her bond to her baby. Men have no such advantage. They tend to feel guilty that they don't feel as gooey over everything the baby says and does. There's a reason you're different from her. The goal of all male-dom is *not* to become like females.

I speak in generalities here and again refer to dummy lights. Women are generally more relationship oriented than men. That means they know what's going on well before you do. They raise the alarm. You tend to ignore it. The point of your differences is that you need to listen to her, but listen with discernment and leadership. Your natural instincts are also necessary in raising children. She'll be tender right to the point of exhaustion and enabling. You need to call a halt.

Dummy lights raise a question. Investigate the problem, don't react. Find the appropriate solution. If she's enabling because she's exhausted, then give her a break until she's strong enough to handle it again. If she's enabling because she doesn't know a better way, then try something different. Lead.

When you were little, the infant who slept through the night at four weeks began wanting to play in the middle of the night at nine months. I kept getting up. I was exhausted. After many nights, my husband put his arm gently on me and quietly said, *"He will go back to sleep."* He was right. The crying lasted only briefly and all-night sleeping was resumed. The two of you are in charge together, not the children. You both have contributions to make. Keep up the good work.

STEPS:

1. Look at your parent's parenting style. Just as your personality isn't a perfect type, neither is your parenting style. Nobody is a perfect type, so rate where your parents were Authoritative, Authoritarian, and Permissive. Share your stories. Discuss what you think your style is. Review personality types. *Please Understand Me* has a great section on how the different personality types parent. (See Appendix II)

2. Set parenting goals annually.

3. A rule of thumb in construction is that you step back from your work every hour to see how it's shaping up. When we're too close to our work we don't see when things get out of plumb until they're way out of true. In such a case, the pizza delivery boy arrives and asks, *"Hey! Did you mean for that window to be crooked?"* The same is true with parenting.

Step back and look objectively at how things are going. You'll spot problems before they get so far out of whack that even the pizza delivery kid can diagnose a problem. There are stages to a child's growth, just as there are stages in a marriage. Read a child development book together so you can anticipate the stages of growth of your children. Then make goals to disciple your children through those stages. It's a lot less work than letting things get out of control, then trying to fix the problems.

4. Couples sometimes have children in an attempt to fix a weak marriage. It doesn't work. Marriage is meant to support children. Children are not meant to support marriage.

Commit to each other to keep your marriage strong. Family life has a way of keeping parents so busy that they neglect each other. When the children leave home, two strangers are left living together. It takes work not to let that happen. Do it. Keep your marriage alive. Identify times you're lonely. Identify times when you're too busy for each other. Brainstorm ways to keep your connection to each other vital. Write them down. Do them regularly. Re-write them often.

5. Affirm each other. Celebrate another tune-up completed.

CHAPTER 28

Tune-ups #10-50
Smooth Running to the End

Mileage: Whatever regular schedule you and your bride decide on.

Goal: To have a fulfilling, lasting, mutually supporting, healthy marriage.

You're never "done" with tune-ups. Because we all change as we grow older, we need to re-visit all of the above to check the systems and make sure they fit who we are today. Set aside an annual check-up where you set goals, check on each other, and celebrate.

CAUTION: Never do tune-ups or maintenance on a birthday, anniversary, or Valentine's Day. Those days should always be days of celebration. Don't attach a work memory on her wiring or in your components.

In the first few years of marriage, there are more adjustments to be made than after twenty years. If adjustments are made in an atmosphere of safety, security, and commitment, they become so much easier. If adjustments are attempted while under stress, things which may have bent often break. That's why you do this stuff when everything is going well. Don't wait for the crisis to force the review.

"Whoever wants to be a leader among you must be your servant."[1] Being the head of a family doesn't translate to having power to make others do what you want. It translates to responsibility for and to those under your care.

When you accept your role as servant instead of benevolent dictator you'll find life much easier.

Why? What does the inconsistency mean? I've always thought of women and children as the ecological equivalent of an indicator species for the health of society. When the women get hard, tough, and/or profane and the children follow that lead, we, as a culture, and as families, are in trouble.

Please **Note:** I said hard, not strong. Both sexes can aspire to being strong without becoming tough.

Don't skimp on the tools. Quality tools are worth the cost. Time is your most valuable tool. Remember you're wanting a lifetime guarantee. You won't get it by devoting the least possible effort.

Note: Celebrate often. Don't wait for the raise or promotion. Remember the point system when you were little? Why should I give you one measly point for doing the dishes when I could give you 101 or 1,000? It didn't cost anymore to give you 1,000 points than it did to give you one point, but it sure made a difference in how praised you felt. We used any excuse for a point. In the same way, flowers don't have to be used only on birthdays or anniversaries. Candy doesn't have to be an entire box. It can be one piece. For fun, give a trophy or a wall plaque. If you hate buying cards, then bite the bullet and buy a bunch of them at one time. Then they're already at hand when you want to give them during the year.

Remember when your friend bought a bag of Hershey Kisses and some flowers? When his girlfriend came home there was a line of Kisses on the floor leading to the flowers and a note saying, *"I kiss the ground you walk on."*

When your bride gets a promotion, faces a conflict, or earns a degree, buy a Skor bar. Then celebrate, celebrate, celebrate.

Note: Maintenance for a vehicle and for a wife have very different outcomes. No matter how well you take care of a vehicle, it won't last forever. Maintenance on a wife, however doesn't just keep her from falling apart; it helps her grow and get better.

I watched two guys load a trackhoe onto a trailer. It was a great picture of marriage. One guy was in the trackhoe—a giant, hulking, strong piece of equipment. The other guy was defenseless on the ground, well within harm's way. They both depended on each other for safety. The guy on the ground was in danger as the hoe arm swung around him to be in position on the trailer. Once the equipment was on the trailer, though, the guy in the big strong thing was in peril. If loaded wrong, it could easily tip.

The guys put their lives in each other's hands. The guy with the power of the equipment puts his life in the hands of the guy on the ground who signals how far to back up and when to turn. Once on the trailer, the trackhoe puts the bucket on the ground and lifts the side on the trailer up. The man on the ground climbs under the bucket and removes the blocks from under the trailer. They trust each other. They depend on each other. They take risks for each other. They succeed when each one does the work of serving the other.

In marriage we need to recognize that our lives—emotional, physical, spiritual, and mental—are in each other's hands. We need to have trust in *all* four areas. We need to serve each other instead of trying to get something from each other. That means that men *and* women need to ask aloud, *"How am I doing? How am I affecting your physical, emotional, mental, and spiritual safety?"*

Love covers a multitude of sins, but *you can't take it for granted.* You can lose it. Love is living, and as long as it's living, it covers. When it begins to shrivel, it exposes. When love begins to die, you see with critical eyes.

Love is not one step. It's all the maintenance and tune-ups. Love grieves the nicks to your relationship, but loves in spite of them. It knows her and accepts her nuances as endearing, like when guys talk about a favorite old vehicle. *"Yep, that old Ford I had, in order to start her, you really had to pump the gas. But once she got going, she was a great old car."*

If love is a living thing, then it also needs nourishment. If nourishment is meted out, living becomes just surviving. There are marriages that just survive. When nourishment is abundant, living things thrive. You can't have "thriving" without doing the nourishing. The outcome is your choice, your goal.

Getting hurt comes with loving. You can't have one without the other. Trying to protect yourself by being aloof or indifferent doesn't work. Being unforgiving or judgmental doesn't protect you. You're going to hurt whether you love or hate. Hate seems like a strong word, but indifference and being aloof are just mild forms of it. If you choose the negative, your life is always going to be negative. If you choose the positive, your life will have a balance of both positive and negative. The only path to the positive of love is by risking the negatives of hurt. You can't have both. You can't protect yourself *and* enjoy the fullness of love.

Remembering all this stuff is tough. You're not going to remember unless you give yourself some helps. I opened the car door the other day and saw the oil change sticker. Why is the sticker there? Because who remembers the mileage of the last oil change? We forget. It's important to remember, so we write the number on a sticker and put it where we'll see it and be reminded. It's a positive tool, not one that says, *"You dummy! Can't even remember your own mileage, eh?"*

Get some stickers. Use them as a Note-to-Self on when the last date was, when the last romantic event was, when you last reviewed her goals, personality, values, etc. Use them in the areas you find most difficult to remember, not because you're a lousy husband and can't remember important things about your wife, but because your wife and marriage are important to you and you'll do whatever it takes to help you stay on top of the details. Stick it where you'll be reminded—like in the door of your truck.

Note: The key to success in all the above is ninety-percent attitude.

Hubby: "One of my favorite phrases when I hear a young husband complaining about his wife is, *"You won't say that to your second wife!"* It brings them up short, making them realize they need to re-think their attitude and subsequent behavior."

In the world of real vehicles there are a finite number of makes and models.

Two guys can actually own the same vehicle. They can go to a website and get accurate help. The vehicle metaphor breaks down here. No two guys are going to have the same make and model of wife. The Well-Duh is that when your Chevy isn't running right you don't turn to the diesel guy to ask advice. You *know* that, so don't turn to the nearest guy and ask him what to do about your marriage. There are an infinite number of wife makes and models out there. This manual, once you've filled in the blanks and done the work, is specific to *your* model. That's what makes it work, unlike books about Venus and Mars. You can't ask another guy, even if he writes relationship books. He doesn't understand *his* model, let alone yours! So you and your "model" need to take time to fill in the blanks together.

Don't try to do all the maintenance or tune-ups at once any more than you try to do all the maintenance and tune-ups in the car manual at once. Just be sure to celebrate after you change the oil. Celebrate after you rotate the tires. Celebrate after you've blown a gasket and the new gasket has your marriage purring again.

This manual isn't everything you need to know. This isn't a book on parenting or conflict resolution, or making wise choices, or faith, or all the other subjects you encounter in life. This is just what I felt was most important for you to know that we didn't cover while you lived at home. Now it's your turn to take the tools you've been given and build a marriage that you want to pass on to your children.

I'm *really* proud of you for making it to this page,

Mom

SECTION 4
MISCELLANEOUS

CHAPTER 29

Extreme Driving Conditions

THE OBVIOUS THING to say here is: if I could, I'd protect you from *Extreme Driving Conditions.* But I wouldn't. I wish they didn't exist. I wish the world was a perfect place. However, *Extreme Driving Conditions* taught me to be honest instead of nice. They gave me a backbone. They gave me courage and confidence and skills for handling tough situations. I grew up. I wouldn't want anything less for you. Instead, I'll tell you that you have the character to face *Extreme Driving Conditions* and become stronger.

Note: *Extreme Driving Conditions* can be due to excessive heat or cold, stop and go driving—feeling like you're not getting anywhere—idling for long periods, rough roads, dusty driving conditions, steep hills. Remember that steep hills are not only difficult to climb, but can be tricky to come down as well. Carrying heavy loads of success *or* failure puts strain on life. There's no path through life paved entirely with smooth roads. Make one of your routine check-up periods a planning time for rough roads. The best preparation you can make is in yourself.

The old saying is that you either become bitter or better. Marriage, like parenting, is unfortunately something you don't need to qualify for. Any idiot can go out, say, "*I do,*" and head down the road.

Know that problems will come your way. Sometimes it'll be your choice that brings on crisis and conflict. Other times it'll be her choice that takes you down a rough patch. Sometimes it'll be other drivers on the road, other passengers, pedestrians, the weather, stray animals or even the road itself.

Arguing about who got us into the mess doesn't solve the problem. You don't solve people, you do solve problems. You get through tough times if you go together, depend on each other, and share your strengths instead of using them against each other. It takes a lot of practice, and believe me, life will send you quite a bit of it.

So prepare for *Extreme Driving Conditions* by forgiving each other—practice it weekly, monthly, daily, if necessary. If you practice it on little things, everyday things, you won't choke on it quite so much on the big things.

Tell your children when they become men or women so they don't have to go out and prove it to themselves or depend on someone else to tell them. Tell them why you consider them men or women—not adult, not mature, but men or women. They wonder anyway: *Is it because I have sexual urges? Is it because I can drive, drink, date, hold down a job? Is it because I can have a baby?* Sadly, our culture doesn't make a ceremony of adulthood. So make your own ceremony. Make it around age 13. Then for pity's sake, give them adult responsibilities. Tell them where they have good judgment that you trust. Put them in family roles of leadership and follow *them* for a change. Let them fail.

You can't be a success in life if you never learn how to overcome mistakes. Failing is part of learning. If making mistakes is wrong, then learning won't happen for fear of failing. Turn life over to them while they're still under your roof so you can show them how to make course corrections.

Sex is one of the poorest harbingers of having arrived. Children get abused too often. They're still children even though an older person (I refuse to call them adults) has tagged them for adult activities. Being an adult has to be defined in a much broader view. When it isn't, either by the family or by our culture, sex and having babies becomes the defining moment of being man and woman. We as a culture can do so much better than that.

I know this looks like I've switched from how to understand women to parenting. How the two of you were parented brings a great deal of potential into your marriage. If simply getting physical distance between us and our parents eliminated all the weakness of parenting, then none of us would have baggage, yet *we all do.*

As you become parents, how your parents parented will become more a part of your marriage. One reason the sins of the fathers tend to be passed on to the children, to the third and fourth generation, is that nobody stops to figure out why they do what they do.

One story I enjoy is about a family recipe for ham. The recipe called for cutting off the end of the ham. One generation after another cut off the end before baking the ham. Finally one daughter asked "*Why?*" Grandma answered, "*Oh! My pan wouldn't hold a whole ham so we always cut off the end to make it fit.*"

We do what we do because it was done to us. We make the choice of passing on our history intact or modified. Parenting is part of the *Extreme Driving Conditions* you'll travel over.

I remember the day we brought you home from the hospital. I held your tiny, innocent, sleeping form in my arms and felt overwhelmed. I was going to mess up. I knew it. No matter how hard I tried, no matter how much I loved you, I knew there was no way I could be perfect. Every time I made a mistake, you were going to suffer the consequences. Blame wasn't going to help. It doesn't solve problems. So I asked your forgiveness right then and decided that I would keep being honest and asking your forgiveness when I made mistakes. I also forgave my parents for their mistakes. Suddenly, I was just as inexperienced as they were.

A word about parenting mistakes. Children often grow up making vows. "*When I'm grown up, I won't make my children _____.*" For me, one of the memorable issues was getting to sit behind the door for hours, thrumming the springy door stop. The noise drove my dear mother nuts. I decided that when *I* grew up, *my* kids could sit behind the door and play with that silly door stop all they wanted. I remember the long anticipated day I sat you down and showed you the delight of making the door stop spring go, "thoinggggggg." You looked at it and promptly crawled off to do something better.

Our children are not us. What was important to me was not important to you and it's legitimate. What was important to my parents wasn't important to me. It isn't a rejection of family: it's a declaration of personhood. In order to have healthy marriages, we have to be individuals in our own right. Sometimes we've married another person hoping they'd fill in our missing part and make us whole. It doesn't work for long, and then here come those *Extreme Driving Conditions*. When one weak person is carried by the stronger one, there isn't much flexibility for *Extreme Driving Conditions* and the relationship tends to break.

Remember how I said that the most important assaults on your marriage come from within instead of without? Like driving, obvious threats to your marriage are easy to avoid. You see an elk in the road and you automatically try to miss it. It's what you've been staring at on the road all your life that suddenly becomes a weakness when the road demands more from you.

Family is great. It's vital. But the world doesn't do everything the way your family did. Often you'll be no more successful in the world than your family was, unless you choose to overcome what they didn't before they let you go out the door with your own set of keys. Each generation needs to do this re-evaluation. I can't emphasize it enough. Family values are wonderful. They're necessary. But if family values aren't tweaked with each generation, we'll still be cutting the ham the way our grandparents did and won't be able to relate to our own culture.

CAUTION: When I say family values need to be tweaked, I'm not talking about core values of honesty, integrity, family time, etc. I'm talking about whether the meals are home-cooked or the laundry is hung on the line. Whether dad washes the car and changes the oil or if mom does. Preserve your heritage by keeping it relevant to your world.

Note: You will make mistakes. Do-over as often as necessary.

CHAPTER 30

Insurance Policy and Driver's License

MILEAGE: TWICE A year.

Goal: To keep God at the core of your marriage.

As I said earlier, you have to take care of what you value or it gets lost. This principle is as true about your relationship with God as with your wife.

Whoa. I can hear it now. What's God got to do with understanding women? What does my relationship with God have to do with my relationship with my wife? Don't get preachy on me here!

I'll do my best to tell you how it can work, not how you have to do it. Whatever your faith is, it affects how you relate to people and that includes your marriage.

When you marry, you made a vow to each other *and* to God. You were *"joined together in the sight of God."* He was given a vital part of your relationship. Turning to God only during crisis won't build up your marriage.

Your relationship with God is your safety equipment. He's the ABS braking system, the airbag, the spare tire, and the fire extinguisher. Your commitment to Him and His place of relevance in your life needs to be checked regularly, just as you need to check that the spare tire is inflated and the fire extinguisher is charged.

How are God and marriage connected? Marriage is meant to be an earthly experience of what it means to be in relationship with God. God uses words like *"marriage banquet, bridegroom,* and *bride"* to reveal His delight in us. He wants a relationship of love and celebration. He makes pledges to us of faithfulness and loyalty. He wants the union to last forever—way beyond *"till death do us part."*

God tells us the way to have this intimate relationship with Him is by loving Him with all of our heart, soul, and strength, and committing to life with Him. It's the same promise you made to your bride when you said *"I do."*

Ahh—I sense a wail out there. *It's too hard!* In fact, it's impossible! *Nobody* can love God with all of their heart, soul, and strength, *and* commit one hundred percent to Him. Let's go back to your marriage for a moment. When you stood up, exchanged rings, got all dewy–eyed, and eager to celebrate life together, can you imagine standing there and saying, "Well, I love you, but I can't give you *all* of myself. You can have eighty-two percent of my heart. My soul? Well, how about forty-five percent? And my strength? Well, tonight, baby, it's all yours, but I can't promise it's yours *all* the time."

We have good intentions when we say *"I do"* both to each other and to God. The promise isn't that you'll perform perfectly, but that each time anything less is given you won't blow it off.

We aren't any more perfect at the altar when we say *'I do"* than we are when we say *"I do"* to God. Our imperfection doesn't stop us from getting married. Don't let it stop you from working on your relationship with God. The bombardment of self and the daily grind shoves us off course just a little bit every day. Without regular course correction, we get way off course.

So how do we stay faithful to our *"I do"* promise? There are two steps. The first is love and the second is commitment. Love has three components: heart, soul, and strength. We need to be aware of all three. We don't commit only our intellect to marriage.

Don't get hung up with the wrong goal here. The goal isn't perfection, with God or with each other. The goal is a growing relationship, which comes from making mistakes and asking forgiveness. A relationship that doesn't have mistakes is one where somebody doesn't feel safe enough to take risks, to be honest.

God tells us His love is perfect. Perfect love eliminates fear.[1] Fear keeps us from wholeheartedly committing. Fear also keeps us from loving unreservedly. The sad thing is that the walls we erect for self-protection end up isolating us from the very love we crave instead of protecting us from the hurt we fear. The walls had to come down in order to enjoy marriage. They have to come down in order to enjoy God.

Let's look at the other part of that instruction, commitment. Relationship, with a wife and with God, requires both love *and* commitment.

Love with commitment has to be self-sacrificing. I'm not talking about nebulous, kick-me-in-the-pants stuff. Commitment isn't dysfunctional. It's a careful, determined choice to participate in relationship come what may. It has to say, *"When I don't love you, I'm still committed to you."*

Love changes over the years. Love may seem to disappear altogether, only to emerge on the other side of a storm more beautiful than ever. Love without commitment will never see blessings on the other side. It'll only see the storm and its damage. Christ's love on the other side of the cross is even more beautiful than His love as a good man on this side of the cross.

So, how do you evaluate this love/commitment safety equipment? Think of equalizers on the car stereo. Mentally, run the toggle switch up to the level you think you have. As with the equalizer in the car, you can move the slide up and down all day and it doesn't matter. You have to turn on the music and listen for distortion. You're going to have to ask questions and get feedback. The feedback may annoy your ears, but if you don't make changes, the feedback doesn't just go away. Keep tweaking until your relationship is music to your ears.

So what does this loving with "all my heart, soul, and strength" look like? God defines what your love for her needs to look like—it's sacrificial. It has the goal of helping her become the best *she* can be, not making your life as comfortable as *you* want it to be. Using your strength *for* her makes you more powerful, not less. This doesn't mean she gets her own way. Use your strength to make her better, not to enable her weakness.

All this talk of sacrifice also raises the issue of What About Me? When you're giving your all to doing life the way God wants, what comes back at you more than makes up for the self-sacrifice. While you're sacrificing for her, she's meant to be sacrificing for you. And while you're both obeying God, He's honoring your obedience.

Note: I didn't just promise that life would be rosy. God isn't a good luck charm you rub the right way and get what you want. The blessing He gives may simply be peace of mind and heart.

We're only human. We tend to forget. God wants us to write down what He tells us and review it often.[2] It's the same pattern with your mate—if we don't **write** down our reasons for commitment, **review** those reasons at least once a year, and **tell** our mates the basis for our commitment, we'll forget. Our bride will come to her own conclusions based on our actual behavior.

Wholehearted commitment to God is a daily reality, just as it is with marriage. *You must love the Lord your God with all your heart, all your soul, and all your strength, <u>and</u> you must commit yourselves wholeheartedly to these commands.*[3] (emphasis mine.)

I wish Christians and churches were perfect, but they aren't and they aren't ever going to be. You can't take a man from a non-believing way of life, hand him a Bible, and expect total change. It can take a lifetime to complete his divorce from a former commitment to a way of heart, soul, and strength. A person is a lot to transform, and perfection just doesn't happen. *"I'm sorry"* has to be said often in marriage and to God.

Marriage love is the kind of relationship God wants with us. He's the only third party in your marriage who will increase your love for your mate the more you love Him. He is the only third party who has your best interests at heart. Update your safety in Him regularly and often, as often as it takes.

When commitment is wholeheartedly given, to God or to spouse, the transformation is miraculous. I watched this happen to a co-worker, Sam. He was a very immature playboy who regaled us with his weekend antics. Then he met Angie. He committed to marriage and was transformed. He matured, handled increasing responsibility at work, was given respect, and quickly advanced in the work place. A person we hadn't particularly enjoyed being around became someone we looked forward to working with. He was still the same age, the same bundle of personality and life experience. The only thing that changed was his commitment to something other than himself.

We all mean it when we say *"I do."* but daily life reveals where we withhold some of heart, a bit of body, and a modicum of soul. It shows we don't know ourselves well. Is my heart, with God and my spouse, one hundred percent or is it seventy-eight percent? How about my soul? My strength? Where your commitment isn't one hundred percent is where stress on the marriage and on your relationship with God will be. This is why the Bible speaks of a man loving his body being a reflection of a healthy relationship. If a man abuses his own body, then he can't love others one hundred percent.

Is your strength hers when she needs it? Is your heart and mind reliably there or is it always circumstantial? *"I'll do it if it doesn't interfere with what I want."* Love sacrifices because it's committed. Uncommitted love doesn't sacrifice. It may enter into unions of similar values and goals, but less than one hundred percent commitment means you don't have all of me. I'm keeping back part for myself. We all do it, most often out of fear from some past hurt or heartache.

You <u>can</u> develop a healthy, robust community that lives right with God and enjoy its results <u>only</u> if you do the hard work of getting along with each other, treating each other with dignity and honor.[4] Being right with God yields the fruit of being right with your mate. In some mystical way, loving God with all of our heart, soul, and strength enhances our ability to love our mate.

This issue of commitment needs to be evaluated in a tune-up. You need to be able to ask and receive an honest answer. Ask, *"How much of my strength do you feel you have? Can you ask for my help with a reasonable expectation of receiving it? Or do I tell you, 'no,' more often than I say, 'yes'?"* Repeat the questions with soul and heart. This isn't meant to be a one way conversation. It's fair to tell each other the way you've tried to please the other daily with your strength. We aren't mind readers. We have to tell each other how often our mate is on our mind. Like it or not, we tend to expect reciprocity. We tend to expect others to reason like we do. Of course, that isn't the real world, but it doesn't keep us from thinking that way. That's why we take time out to remind ourselves how the closest person to me thinks differently than I do. This isn't a time for one-upmanship either.

There's a huge difference between wanting me to be with you and you wanting to be with me. The same is true with God.

Steps:

Spend time figuring out where things have crowded out God. I'm assuming things have interfered because it happens to everyone.

1. Fill in the equalizer chart for your relationship with God, using the letter "G."

EQUALIZER CHART

Percentage	Heart	Soul	Strength	Commitment	Mind
100%					
75%					
50%					
25%					
0%					

2. Fill it in for your relationship with your spouse, using the letter of her name. Why am I mixing in spouse with God here? If your spouse doesn't have a part of you, then God probably doesn't either.

3. Get feedback. Ask questions like, *"Can you ask for my help with a reasonable expectation of receiving it, or do I tell you 'no,' more often than not?"* Ask, *"When I do this for you, do you feel that I'm doing it for you or*

for myself?" "I think of you when I do these jobs. Do you feel loved when you see this effort? What do I do that makes you feel loved?"

4. Take steps to correct your settings:

   a. Measure where your love and strength are being spent now—use the time chart in Appendix III to see where your day—your strength—goes.

   b. Look at your checkbook to see where your commitment, your heart goes.

   c. Grab one piece of wisdom (see below) to focus on daily for the next six months. Carry it in your wallet, just as you do your insurance card. For the second half of the year use another bit of wisdom.

Wisdom:

   a. *Husbands, go all out in love for your wives. Don't take advantage of them.*[5]

   b. *The marriage bed must be a place of mutuality—the husband seeking to satisfy his wife, the wife seeking to satisfy her husband. Marriage is not a place to "stand up for your rights." Marriage is a decision to serve the other, whether in bed or out.*[6]

   c. *Husbands, go all out in your love for your wives, exactly as Christ did for the church—a love marked by giving, not getting. Christ's love makes the church whole. His words evoke her beauty. Everything He does and says is designed to bring the best out of her, dressing her in dazzling white silk, radiant with holiness. And that is how husbands ought to love their wives. They're really doing themselves a favor.*[7]

   d. *No one abuses his own body, does he? No, he feeds and pampers it. That's how Christ treats us, the church, since we are part of His body. And this is why a man leaves father and mother and cherishes his wife. No longer two, they become "one flesh." This is a huge mystery, and I don't pretend to understand it all. What is clearest to me is the way*

Christ treats the church. And this provides a good picture of how each husband is to treat his wife, loving himself in loving her, and how each wife is to honor her husband.[8]

e. *As we live in God, our love grows more perfect.*[9]

f. *But if we love one another, God dwells deeply within us and His love becomes complete in us—perfect love!*[10]

g. *You <u>can</u> develop a healthy, robust community that lives right with God and enjoy its results <u>only</u> if you do the hard work of getting along with each other, treating each other with dignity and honor.*[11] (emphasis mine.)

h. *Everyone who confesses that Jesus is God's Son participates continuously in an intimate relationship with God. We know it so well, we've embraced it heart and soul, this love that comes from God…When we take up a permanent residence in a life of love, we live in God and God lives in us. This way love has the run of the house, becomes at home and mature in us.*[12]

5. Time. *I don't have time.* It's what we all think. You won't get different results unless you change. Fill out a daily log. Figure out where your time goes now. At the end of the week, take time to look over where you've spent time and if your choices reflect your values and goals. If not, the activities you did that didn't support your goals are the places to make changes.

If you ask yourself "*Where did the time go?*" on a weekly basis, you won't wonder where your life went when you're in your fifties. Time is an unrenewable resource. We all have the same twenty-four hours. Spend it wisely.

Every six to twelve months: Update Your Insurance.

Goal: Express appreciation for each other.

In our home, we renew our vehicle insurance twice a year. You might renew only once a year. Whichever is your pattern, renew your marriage insurance that often as well. Every time you make an insurance payment, make a spouse value check. I'm not talking about what her personal values are here. I'm talking about why *you* value *her*.

In order to determine an insurance premium, value has to be given to what you don't want to lose. Affirm her value to you. Please get beyond the, "*Wow, I don't have to cook or go to the Laundromat anymore.*" level of appreciation. Unlike your car, her value to you should appreciate over the years. Re-read *"Johnny Lingo's Eight Cow Wife"* online.

In order to insure something, you have to know the value of what you have, and what it takes to protect it against loss, theft, or damage. Know the value of your relationship so you're willing to guard, defend, protect, and sacrifice to keep it healthy and growing.

When I first married, the divorce rate was 1:4. I sure felt sorry for the other three beside me in my Marriage and Family class. That "one" wasn't going to be me! Twenty-eight years later it was. Now the divorce rate is 1:2. It takes work to not let that "one" be you.

Re-marriage, even to a wonderful person, cannot duplicate a lifetime of shared experiences. Believe me, there's no substitute for reaching fifty with someone who has been there beside you sharing life's experiences. It doesn't matter if your divorce has the approval of both sides of the aisle and the minister who married you. Approval isn't the point. Who was right or wrong doesn't matter. Divorce robs everyone. Divorce leaves long wounds, as you well know. You just can't undo life with one person, take up with another person, and expect to come away with no ill effects.

Value what you have. Insure it regularly.

Steps:

1. Tell her how your appreciation of her has increased in the past six months.

2. Tell her why you appreciate her.

3. Tell her what you don't want to lose. Be specific.

4. Do one thing that demonstrates how much you enjoy the privilege of having her in your life.

5. Tell her why you chose her make and model. (Remember to tell her in her love language.)

6. Reviewing your love story is an important part of appreciation. You'll tend to forget it and the two *"eyes-only-for-you"* people in the wedding album become strangers. Keep the story alive by re-telling it. Tell what attracted you to her the first time you saw her. Tell how you felt on your first date. Tell how you felt when you asked her to marry you, when you met her family for the first time, etc. Tell your kids why you love her, why you chose her. I don't mean for you to re-tell your entire story every six months. Just tell the part that means the most to you at the time. Keep on telling it because what is ignored becomes forgotten, and what is forgotten becomes lost.

Every two years: License.

Goal: A quick check of your skills by an outside agent.

Remember the process of getting your license? First came the learner's permit, then the test, then the license. But it didn't stop there. For the first few years you had to renew every two years. As you accumulated successful driving experience, the license was extended for lengthier periods of time. The same is true with marriage. You also took out a license to be married. Engagement was the learner's permit stage. Having family and friends agree to the union equates to passing the driving test. And for the first few years, you need to review the ordinary basics covered during that initial period: communication, conflict resolution, sex. After awhile, if you pass all those areas, then you can skip the review for longer periods of time. That doesn't mean that you skip it altogether, though. The reason you pass the test is because you made the practices of good relationship a part of normal living.

Steps:

1. Check your vision. Can you see clearly things up close and those in the distance? Do you like the impulse of the moment over careful planning? If you're better at one than the other, then get some help to correct your vision. Then remember to use it when making decisions.

2. Do you remember the basic rules of marriage: romance, conflict resolution, apology, love languages? Re-affirm your commitment to her. Re-affirm your commitment to the guidelines of healthy marriage. Re-affirm your commitment to God being a part of your marriage.

3. Do a marriage check-up. Do the test every time you renew your license. Take action on any areas of revealed weakness. And for pity's sake, answer the questions honestly, not giving the answer you know is right, but you don't actually do.

4. Congratulations! You've completed the manual! You've earned your Master Mechanic Marriage Certificate. Good job!

ABOUT THE AUTHOR

TEACHING SMALL ENGINE repair to boys typifies Cathy's ability to translate complex ideas into useful bits, keep attention focused, and still have fun. Imagine a roomful of little boys, poised in front of their own lawn mower engine, chanting, "Intake! Compression! Power! Exhaust!" with arms and fists cheerleading each stage of a four cycle engine. Nobody got hurt. Some of them even remember the lesson.

Cathy's passion is mentoring people by translating everyday events into teachable moments whether speaking at women's retreats, presiding in Toastmasters, Parents Club, church committees, Sunday school, school district talented and gifted committee, or participating on a state committee for the National Alliance for the Mentally Ill. Male professionals dominated her Toastmasters group and elected her to serve as President. The adult Sunday school class she taught included most of the male leadership of the church.

Her passion for teaching comes with a passion for learning. Cathy's degrees are in biology and medical technology, but that didn't stop her from learning to be a midwife to 200 ewes on her ranch, build floats for the Pasadena Rose Parade, write and teach a community college curriculum on empty nest, or write a community newsletter for five years. Her first real job as a medical technologist was diagnosing syphilis for the state of Kansas. She only looks meek and mild-mannered.

Cathy's introduction to the world of vehicles began at birth. Her father raced hard tops until an accident forced his retirement. Then he switched to waving the checkered flag on the racetrack as cars roared by. Cathy went to the races, even acting as a five year old trophy girl after one race.

Her father's friends filled her home with talk of cars and engines all her life. Being an only child in a largely male family meant she went with the guys for test drives and to check out vehicles. In her tight-knit family, one cousin owns a wrecking yard; another built a motorcycle featured on the cover of a motorcycle magazine. Another cousin restores vehicles. At family gatherings, the talk is always about vehicles.

Operating a construction company on the Oregon Coast with her husband and son continues to give Cathy plenty of experience communicating in a man's world.

APPENDIX I
NOTES

Dedication

1. Galatians 5:6b New International Version

Acknowledgments

1. Psalm 102:18, The Message
2. Ephesians 3:20, The New Testament in Modern English, JB Phillips

Chapter 2

1. 1 Corinthians 13: 4-7 paraphrase
2. Galatians 5:6b, New International Version
3. Ephesians 4: 26 The Message
4. 2 Samuel 11
5. Galatians 6:5 New Living Translation
6. Ephesians 5:25-28 The Message

Chapter 3

1. DISC, Marston, William M. (1928). *Emotions of Normal People*. K. Paul, Trench, Trubner & Co. ltd. pp. 405. See Appendix III
2. Keirsey Temperament Sorter, Keirsey, David (May 1, 1998) [1978]. *Please Understand Me II: Temperament, Character, Intelligence* (1st Ed. ed.). Prometheus Nemesis Book Co. ISBN 1885705026.

3. http://smalley.cc/free-personality-test
4. Ephesians 4:6-7, The Message

Chapter 4

1. Numbers 22

Chapter 5

1. Proverbs 10:19 New International Version
2. Ephesians 4:15 paraphrase
3. Lamentations 3:22 paraphrase

Chapter 6

1. 1 Peter 4:8

Chapter 7

1. Galatians 6:4-5 The Message
2. Galatians 6:1 The Message
3. 1 Corinthians 11:3 The Message
4. 1 Corinthians 12: 1-3 The Message
5. Galatians 6:12 The Message
6. Galatians 6:15 The Message
7. Galatians 6:5 The Message
8. Ephesians 5:21 New International Version

Chapter 8

1. *Haynes Automotive Repair Manual,* page 0-17, volume 30010, 1994, Curt Choate, Mike Stubblefield, and John H Haynes, Haynes North America, Inc. ISBN 1 56392 132 4
2. I Corinthians 13:4-8, New International Version
3. *Haynes Automotive Repair Manual,* page 0-17, volume 30010, 1994,

Curt Choate, Mike Stubblefield, and John H Haynes, Haynes North America, Inc. ISBN 1 56392 132 4

4. Ephesians 5:25-28 The Message

5. *Haynes Automotive Repair Manual,* page 0-17, volume 30010, 1994, Curt Choate, Mike Stubblefield, and John H Haynes, Haynes North America, Inc. ISBN 1 56392 132 4

Chapter 9

1. *Haynes Automotive Repair Manual,* page 0-18, volume 30010, 1994, Curt Choate, Mike Stubblefield, and John H Haynes, Haynes North America, Inc. ISBN 1 56392 132 4

2. Mike Burgess

3. *Haynes Automotive Repair Manual,* page 0-18, volume 30010, 1994, Curt Choate, Mike Stubblefield, and John H Haynes, Haynes North America, Inc. ISBN 1 56392 132 4

4. *Haynes Automotive Repair Manual,* page 0-18, volume 30010, 1994, Curt Choate, Mike Stubblefield, and John H Haynes, Haynes North America, Inc. ISBN 1 56392 132 4

5. 1 Corinthians 13:13 NIV

Chapter 10 Conversion Factors

1. Cannon Beach Christian Conference Center, Womack Conference http://www.cbcc.net/

Chapter 11 Troubleshooting

1. Romans 15:1-2 paraphrase

2. Romans 12:2 paraphrase

3. Romans 8:28, Isaiah 61:3

4. *Haynes Automotive Repair Manual,* page 0-21, volume 30010, 1994, Curt Choate, Mike Stubblefield, and John H Haynes, Haynes North America, Inc. ISBN 1 56392 132 4

5. *Haynes Automotive Repair Manual,* page 0-21, volume 30010, 1994,

Curt Choate, Mike Stubblefield, and John H Haynes, Haynes North America, Inc. ISBN 1 56392 132 4

6. *Haynes Automotive Repair Manual,* page 0-21, volume 30010, 1994, Curt Choate, Mike Stubblefield, and John H Haynes, Haynes North America, Inc. ISBN 1 56392 132 4

7. *Haynes Automotive Repair Manual,* page 0-21, volume 30010, 1994, Curt Choate, Mike Stubblefield, and John H Haynes, Haynes North America, Inc. ISBN 1 56392 132 4

8. *Haynes Automotive Repair Manual,* page 0-21, volume 30010, 1994, Curt Choate, Mike Stubblefield, and John H Haynes, Haynes North America, Inc. ISBN 1 56392 132 4

9. *Haynes Automotive Repair Manual,* page 0-21, volume 30010, 1994, Curt Choate, Mike Stubblefield, and John H Haynes, Haynes North America, Inc. ISBN 1 56392 132 4

10. *Haynes Automotive Repair Manual,* page 0-21, volume 30010, 1994, Curt Choate, Mike Stubblefield, and John H Haynes, Haynes North America, Inc. ISBN 1 56392 132 4

11. *Haynes Automotive Repair Manual,* page 0-21, volume 30010, 1994, Curt Choate, Mike Stubblefield, and John H Haynes, Haynes North America, Inc. ISBN 1 56392 132 4

12. *Haynes Automotive Repair Manual,* page 0-21, volume 30010, 1994, Curt Choate, Mike Stubblefield, and John H Haynes, Haynes North America, Inc. ISBN 1 56392 132 4

13. *Haynes Automotive Repair Manual,* page 0-21, volume 30010, 1994, Curt Choate, Mike Stubblefield, and John H Haynes, Haynes North America, Inc. ISBN 1 56392 132 4

14. *Haynes Automotive Repair Manual,* page 0-21, volume 30010, 1994, Curt Choate, Mike Stubblefield, and John H Haynes, Haynes North America, Inc. ISBN 1 56392 132 4

Chapter 12

1. Galatians 6:5
2. 1 Corinthians 13:4-7 paraphrase
3. Galatians 5:6 New International Version

Chapter 13

1. 1 Peter 3:8-12 The Message

Chapter 14

1. 1 Corinthians 13: 4-7 The Message
2. Galatians 5:6 New International Version
3. Ephesians 4:26 The Message

Chapter 15

1. I Corinthians 13: 4-7 paraphrase
2. Colossians 3:19 The Message

Chapter 16

1. American Marketplace Demographics and Spending Patterns, page 517 New Strategist Publications; editorial director Cheryl Russell 9 edition (June 1, 2009) ISBN-10: 193511428X ISBN-13: 978-1935114284

Chapter 18

1. Psalms 19:12 New Living Translation

Chapter 19

1. Webster's New Twentieth Century Dictionary Unabridged, Second Edition, page 1968, Simon & Schuster Publishers, copyright 1983, ISBN 0-671-41819-X

Chapter 22

1. Matthew 18:15-17 The Message
2. James 1:20 New International Version
3. Ephesians 4: 26 JB Phillips
4. Romans 12:19 The Message

5. Matthew 6:14 New Living Translation
6. Colossians 3:19 New Living Translation
7. Ephesians 5:28 New Living Translation
8. Ephesians 4:26 New International Version
9. 1 Samuel 15:11-12
10. 1 Peter 4:8 New International Version
11. 1 Corinthians 13: 4-7 paraphrase
12. Galatians 5:6 New International Version
13. Romans 3:23 New Living Translation

Chapter 24

1. Ephesians 5:25 paraphrase
2. 1Peter 3:7 New Living Translation
3. Ephesians 5:1-2 paraphrase
4. Ephesians 5:25 paraphrase
5. Proverbs 5:18 The Message
6. Ephesians 5:25 The Message
7. Ephesians 5:26-28 The Message
8. Ephesians 5:3-4 The Message

Chapter 25

1. 1Corinthians 13:4-7 paraphrase
2. Galatians 6:5 New Living Translation

Chapter 26

1. Hebrews 10:17 The Message
2. John 9:3 The Message
3. Luke 6:39 New International Version

Chapter 27

1. Matthew 20: 25-26 The Message
2. 1 Chronicles 16:43 The Message

Chapter 28

1. Matthew 20: 25-26 New Living Translation

Chapter 30

1. 1 John 4:17-18 paraphrase
2. Deuteronomy 6:6-9 paraphrase
3. Deuteronomy 6:5 paraphrase
4. James 3:17-18 The Message
5. Colossians 3:19 The Message
6. 1 Corinthians 7:2-6 The Message
7. Ephesians 5:25-28 The Message
8. Ephesians 5:29-33 The Message
9. 1 John 4:17 New Living Translation
10. 1 John 4:11-12 The Message
11. James 3:17-18 The Message
12. 1 John 4:117-18 The Message

APPENDIX II
RESOURCES

Chapter 3

1. *10 Stupid Things Men Do To Mess Up Their Lives*, Dr. Laura Schlessinger, Cliff Street Books, Harper Collins, 1997
2. *10 Stupid Things Women Do To Mess Up Their Lives*, Dr. Laura Schlessinger, Cliff Street Books, Harper Collins, 1997
3. DiSC® Personality Test
4. *Please Understand Me Character & Temperament Types*, David Keirsey, Marilyn Bates, Prometheus Nemesis Book Company 1978

Chapter 6

1. http://www.cafepress.com/+chocolate+magnets

Chapter 9

1. Cannon Beach Christian Conference Center, Womack Conference http://www.cbcc.net/

Chapter 6

1. http://www.cafepress.com/+chocolate+magnets

Chapter 21

1. *The Marriage Checkup Questionnaire* [Paperback] H. Norman Wright, Gospel Light Publishers, ISBN-10: 0830730648 ISBN-13: 978-0830730643, 2002

Chapter 24

1. *Boundaries When to Say YES, When to Say NO to Take Control of Your Life,* Dr. Henry Cloud, Dr. John Townsend, Zondervan, 1992
2. *The Five Languages of Apology How to Experience Healing in All Your Relationships,* Gary Chapman, Jennifer Thomas, Northfield Publishing, 2006
3. *Money Before Marriage A Financial Workbook for Engaged Couples,* Larry Burkett with Michael E. Taylor, Moody Press 1996

Chapter 25

1. *Boundaries When to Say YES, When to Say NO to Take Control of Your Life,* Dr. Henry Cloud, Dr. John Townsend, Zondervan, 1992
2. *The Five Languages of Apology How to Experience Healing in All Your Relationships,* Gary Chapman, Jennifer Thomas, Northfield Publishing, 2006

APPENDIX III
MAKE, MODEL, AND VIN TESTS

Chapter 3

GOAL SHEET SAMPLE

GOAL: Run the Boston Marathon

STEPS to get there:

Long Term:

Time: one year

Measure: run the marathon

Mid Term:

Time: six months

Measure: run in five local races: Portland, Astoria, Seattle, Hood to Coast, Bald Peak Half

Short Term:

Time: three months

Measure: be able to run ten miles

Time: one month

Measure: be able to run five miles

Time: this week

Measure: run around the track for two miles

Steps:	Who	Deadline
1. Buy good running shoes	me	this week
2. Plot a training route	me	this week
3. Plot a 26 week training schedule	me	this week
4. Get running partners	me	this week
5. Sign up	me	this week
6. Buy plane ticket	me	August, next year
7. Make lodging reservation	me	August, next year
8. Train	me	Saturday
9. Run in five local races	me	over next six months
10. Establish qualifying time	me	April, next year
11. Follow training diet – Engine 2 Diet	me	today

TIME MANAGEMENT SURVEY

Indicate how often the following statements are true:

1. I don't have time to do the things I need to do	Usually	Sometimes	Never
2. I don't have time to do the things I want to do	Usually	Sometimes	Never
3. I feel pressured by all the things I have to do.	Usually	Sometimes	Never
4. I feel out of control because of all the demands on my time.	Usually	Sometimes	Never

5.	I have lots of good ideas but it seems that something always gets in the way so I haven't accomplished a lot of things I would like to	Usually	Sometimes	Never
6.	6. I think I'm capable of doing more and I would like to do more but there doesn't seem to be time, or things seem to get in the way.	Usually	Sometimes	Never
7.	I put less into a project than I would like because there isn't enough time.	Usually	Sometimes	Never
8.	I think I would be better off if I could manage my time better.	Usually	Sometimes	Never
9.	My life is perfect and I'm accomplishing everything I want, and I still have plenty of time to relax.	Usually	Sometimes	Never

DiSC Mechanics

Read the following descriptions. Mark the traits that describe you most accurately. None of us fit in one category 100%. Find the category that has the most marks and write it down on the page in Chapter 3. Remember this is not a complete personality test. This gives you basic information to start with.

D – Do It!

Dominant, **D**irect, **D**emanding, **D**ecisive

strong and aggressive think Lion

Cummins Diesel 5.9 GM Duramax

Motivation: challenge and control

Values: freedom from control, authority, difficult assignments, chances for advancement, choices, variety, competition, power, taking risks

Favorite sayings: you're not the boss of me, Do it, show me the money, what's it going to cost, get to the point

Works best with spouse who provides: direct answers, keeps on task, gets to the point, freedom for personal accomplishment

Has a hard time remembering: to relax, that people are important, rules are important, self-discipline is important, finishing is important, people's feelings need to be considered, money isn't everything

Jim Entler

I - Fantastic

Inspiring, **I**nfluencing, **I**mpressing, **I**nducing

Impressive, loves attention, flashy think Otter

TR, MG, Jag, 409, Corvette Z06

Motivation: recognition and approval

Values: prestige, relationships, freedom from details, helping others, motivating others, sharing ideas, adventure

Favorite sayings: TA-DA, Look at ME! FANTASTIC!

Works best with a spouse who: is fair and a friend, active socially, praises, rewards behavior

Has a hard time remembering: being on time, optimism isn't always the answer, being responsible is more important than being popular, to listen, to meet deadlines.

Jim Entler

S – Harmony

Submissive, **S**teady, **S**table

steady, good all around, think golden retriever

Chevy 350

Motivation: security, stability, and support

Values: accomplishment, routine, belonging to groups, security, order, relationships, listening, harmony

Favorite sayings: May I help? Are you okay? Let's get along.

Works best with a spouse who: is relaxed and friendly, gives time to adjust to changes, encourages him/her to work at own pace, is supportive

Has a hard time remembering: change is necessary, honesty is more important than relationship, you're not responsible for everyone, discipline is necessary, taking risks is necessary.

Jim Entler

C - Hmmmmm

Competent, **C**ompliant, **C**autious, **C**alculating

independent, hard-working, think beaver

Briggs & Stratton, Cummins Diesel turbo

Motivation: quality and correctness

Values: details, clearly defined tasks, few risks, time to think, work requiring precision and planning

Favorite Sayings: Let me think about that, Hmmmmm, I have an idea, Is this how you want it done? I was thinking…

Works best with a spouse who: listens to suggestions, provides necessary items to do task correctly, spells out details, offers reassurance

Has a hard time remembering: the job needs to get done, perfection isn't always the goal, total support isn't always possible, thorough explanation isn't everything, to look on the positive side

Jim Entler

Different Ways of Looking at Personality

System				Four Personality Types
DiSC	Dominance	Influence	Steadiness	Cautious
Gary Smalley	Lion	Otter	Golden Retriever	Beaver
Winnie the Pooh	Rabbit	Tigger	Pooh	Eeyore
Hippocrates	Choleric	Sanguine	Phlegmatic	Melancholy
D.E.S.A.	Dominant	Expressive	Solid	Analytical
Charlie Brown Characters	Lucy	Snoopy	Charlie Brown	Linus
Biblical Characters	Paul	Peter	Abraham	Moses
Jim Entler	Do It!	TaDa!	Harmony	Hmmmmm
Cathy's System	Cummins Diesel 5.9, GM Duramax	TR, MG, Jag, 409, Corvette Z06	Chevy 350	Briggs & Stratton Cummins Diesel turbo

Values

Personal Values Grid: 1) Eliminate five values. 2) Then eliminate five more values, 3) Then five more until you have your core, can't-live-without five values.

Accomplishment	Adventure	Affection	Approval	Challenge
Competition	Education	Faith	Family	Financial Security
Freedom	Health	Honor	Honesty & Integrity	Independence
Leadership	Loyalty	Order	Perseverance	Pleasure
Prestige	Power	Recognition	Relationship	Respect
Security	Self-Acceptance	Self-Development	Self-Discipline	Spiritual
Vision	Wealth	Wisdom	Work Ethic	

Your Values:_____

Her Values:_____

Marriage Values:_____

Family Values:_____

Chapter 9

Keep a log of your activities to see if where you actually spend your time matches where you think you want to spend your time - your values and goals. This is different than a day-timer telling you where to be when. This shows you why you don't have the time to do what you think you want to do.

Time	Monday	Tuesday	Wednesday	Thursday	Friday	Saturday	Sunday
5:00 AM							
5:30							
6:00							
6:30							
7:00							
7:30							
8:00							
8:30							
9:00							
9:30							
10:00							
10:30							
11:00							
11:30							
12:00							
12:30							
1:00							
1:30							
2:00							
2:30							
3:00							

3:30							
4:00							
4:30							
5:00							
5:30							
6:00							
6:30							
7:00							
7:30							
8:00							
8:30							
9:00							
9:30							
10:00							
10:30							
11:00							
11:30							

Chapter 10

Concrete Sequential tests – go online or http://www.floatingneutrinos. com/Message/arcs/links_on_abstractrandom.htm

Chapter 12

Go online or - http://www.healthcentral.com/sleep-disorders/stress-test-3454-143.html Also known as the Life Stress Test or the Holmes & Rahe Test

Chapter 13

Go online to the free smiley faces and find the charts that work for you: http://www.bing.com/images/search?q=emotion+chart+smiley+face+pictu res&qpvt=emotion+chart+smiley+face+pictures&FORM=IGRE

Chapter 18

Time chart – see Chapter 3

Chapter 19

Marriage Values Grid: Look at where your values are similar and where they're different from hers. Write down which values you have in common.

Our Values:_____

Family Values Grid: Have each person circle their top five values. Pool the results to find the top values for your family. Recognize your differences as strengths, glad to have that point of view in the family.

Family Values:_____

Personality Test: Gary Smalley http://smalley.cc/free-personality-

Conflict Resolution Agreement Sample: Feel free to cross out and add to this essay. Your agreement has to reflect YOUR values and YOUR personality. Make it as short or as long as you like, just so long as it works for both of you. Test drive it and make revisions as necessary.

CONFLICT RESOLUTION

Sarcasm means to tear flesh – we will speak with courtesy and respect.

We'll let each other speak – no interrupting, no talking over the other.

We'll offer a time of reflection to each other, if needed.

We agree that the purpose of conflict resolution is to fix what is broken so we can be re-united. That means one of us can't win and the other lose. At the end of conflict we will ask if we feel like we won or lost.

We'll own our part of the disagreement.

We'll ask forgiveness.

We'll give forgiveness.

We'll make amends where necessary. We will change behavior where necessary.

Either of us has permission to ask for a time out if the discussion gets too intense.

We will not discuss our disagreement with others – no BS sessions with the guys or the women.

Not all problems can be resolved in one session. We agree to discuss a problem until both of us feel it's resolved.

We'll have a specific goal to be achieved in our conflict. We'll celebrate together when we achieve that goal.

We'll stick to the point, avoiding deflection (what about you!).

We'll work to understand the other's point of view.

We do this because we want a healthy family that brings out the best in both of us; that sets an example for our children and grandchildren to follow; that brings glory to our Savior.

We agree that anger is both healthy and a danger. Our first choice is to not let the sun go down on our anger. Getting the topic out in the open before bedtime is a goal, but not a law. Neither will we let an issue simmer.

In our resolution we will be guided by Scripture, specific to our problem, not in a vague nebulous way. We will not use Scripture to beat each other up, but to build each other up, to correct our thinking.

Chilling silence and raging anger are destructive. Passive/aggressive actions are just as destructive. We'll seek to avoid destructive behaviors.

It's important to know what the disagreement is really about, to get to the heart of the matter, otherwise we'll argue about trivial matters over and over. We agree to get to the heart of the matter.

It may help to list the stresses we each feel – physical, emotional, spiritual, work, family, friends, etc.

We'll affirm our loyalty to each other.

Date: Signed:

Love Languages: see Chapter 8

Chapter 20

See Chapter 3 DiSC

PERSONALITY TYPE DiSC

D = Cummins Diesel 5.9	Lion	DO IT!	Fire, Fire, Fire
I = Corvette – My 409	Otter	Look at ME!	Fire, Ready, Aim
S = Chevy 350	Golden Retriever	HARMONY	Ready, Aim, Fire
C = BMW	Beaver	HMMMM	Aim, Aim, Aim

Chapter 21

Goals – see sample sheet Chapter 3 Appendix III

Chapter 25

Stress Test - See Appendix III, Chapter 12

Chapter 29

Time chart – See Appendix III, Chapter 9

THANKS TO CRITIQUE

You've been an invaluable part of this process. Your encouragement felt unconditional. Your suggestions and honest feedback helped me communicate better. Just the fact that you were here each week kept me writing. Thank you for being part of this process, wherever it may lead.

CPSIA information can be obtained at www.ICGtesting.com
Printed in the USA
BVOW07s1352041113

335301BV00003B/9/P